In the Company of Others

Also by Jory Graham

Chicago: An Extraordinary Guide
Instant Chicago—How to Cope
Katie's Zoo
Children on a Farm
I'm Driving My Analyst Crazy

In the Company of Others

Jory Graham

Harcourt Brace Jovanovich, Publishers
New York and London

Requests for permission to make copies of any part of the work should
be mailed to: Permissions, Harcourt Brace Jovanovich, Publishers,
757 Third Avenue, New York, NY 10017

Library of Congress Cataloging in Publication Data
Graham, Jory, 1923–
In the company of others.
Includes index.
    1. Breast—Cancer—Patients—United States—Biography.
2. Journalists—United States—Biography. 3. Graham, Jory, 1923–
4. Cancer—Social aspects. 5. Cancer—Psychological aspects. I. Title.
RO280.B8G7   362.1'96994'00924 [B]   78-22252
ISBN 0-15-144642-3   AACR2

Printed in the United States of America

First edition

B C D E

To cancer patients everywhere;

To their families, their physicians, their nurses, their friends;

To all of you who have allowed me to share in your individual and unsung acts of courage,

who have taught me so that I may teach others,

who have left glowing private examples of gallantry

for all of us;

To those whose memories are forever part of the human tradition:

Know that I am now, and forever will be so proud to be among you.

Contents

Foreword

Talented observers can teach us a great deal through shared experience; I suppose every one of us dreams of writing a book in which we share our own discoveries and pleasures. *In the Company of Others* shares discoveries, but the experiences it details are harrowing.

I watched this book being lived as it was being written. I have had the unique privilege of working with the author as a writer and as a patient. As one of Jory's physicians (a medical oncologist), I saw chapters finished in the hospital, and have reviewed her newspaper columns while awaiting her blood-test results.

Sometimes a chapter completion merited a small celebration, other times a chapter was itself a sustaining lifeline. But every chapter was a small triumph over time and illness.

From the start, this was a book far removed from the common narrative of "what I did after I found my breast lump." We have seen several such books, magazine articles, and even television movies, and I grant a certain value to them. "Cancer Stories" are almost a genre now, and I am glad that this all-too-common disease is finally becoming less exotic. Still, the one in four Americans who gets cancer faces more than a disease. There is a stigma to this illness. Some diseases imply good things about you—"You work too hard, so you have an ulcer"; "You are too competitive, you'll have a coronary." But cancer victimizes people, and few cancer patients can write books of triumph.

Jory studied cancer, by attending Tumor Board meetings, by reading medical literature for hours at a time, and by questioning her medical consultants. She learned from her newspaper-column readers what their doctors didn't know. Now she shares what she has learned. She teaches cancer to students and to senior physicians. She has lectured to my medical students on numerous occasions, and on each occasion I learned a great deal, too.

I could write the epilogue to this book, for I know what its impact will be. I have seen the effect her weekly column, "A Time for Living," has had. As I read each column in a Chicago Sunday newspaper, I could anticipate my Monday telephone calls. I would guess whether I would receive more calls from patients or physicians. Can I vouch for the medical facts in this book? Yes. Can I expect the majority of physicians to accept it well? No. This paradox is critical to the reader.

Valuable for the patient and for the friend or family member of a patient, *In the Company of Others* is a resource for the physician as well. For, in questioning the elements of the physician-patient relationship, Jory triggers reflection on our role, our ethical obligations, our basic contract with each patient. Some physicians may chide the author for presenting what they interpret as an "anti-doctor" tone. To my colleagues I say that good insights and good advice are often hard to accept but that these are what we need to improve ourselves. Growth is what this book is all about.

John Steinbeck once commented that the professional is always irritated by lay knowledge. In a profile on Jory, *People* magazine softened a story I told their reporter of a colleague who was upset by one of Jory's newspaper columns. His actual remark was, "You're her doctor. Can't you shut her up?" This book is bound to upset some doctors, but I believe it will open up some closed minds.

I am frequently asked, particularly by physicians in training, "Isn't oncology depressing?" I have often found my oncology practice sad, but never depressing. There are numerous "little victories," and occasionally a truly exhilarating moment. I see such a moment in my final re-reading of this book. I see, in Jory's words, "double dares taken and won." Jory says she's "constantly awed by the amount of courage that seriously ill Americans muster." She is a triumph for herself, and for all those who have been helped by her.

John M. Merrill, M.D.
Associate Professor of Clinical Medicine
Northwestern University Medical School
October, 1981

Acknowledgments

I thank the following individuals who shared their knowledge, ideas, and insights throughout the four years I needed to write this book.

Robert G. Addison, M.D.
Grace Aldworth
Joyce Alt, R.N.
George J. Annas, Esq.
Nathaniel I. Berlin, M.D.,
    Ph.D.
Max Boverman, M.D.
Luther W. Brady, M.D.
William N. Brand, M.D.
Edward A. Brunner, M.D.,
    Ph.D.
John Calloway
Donald E. Casey, M.D.
Ned H. Cassem, S.J., M.D.
Robert R. Chilcote, M.D.
William M. Clements, Ph.D.

Mort Crim, L.H.D.
Vincent T. DeVita, Jr., M.D.
Robert J. Eck
Dan C. English, M.D.
Richard A. Evans, M.D.
Herman Feifel, Ph.D.
Frances Lomas Feldman
Justin M. Fishbein
Jayne FitzSimmons, R.N.
Joan Flanagan
Rev. John C. Fletcher, Ph.D.
Max Forman, M.D.
Milt Freudenheim and Betty
    Freudenheim
Melvin V. Gerbie, M.D.
Nancy Gerson

Rev. James L. Gibbons
Audrey K. Gordon
Robert J. Havey, M.D.
Samuel Hellman, M.D.
Robert C. Hickey, M.D.
Raymond W. Houde, M.D.
Robert P. Hudson, M.D.
Norman E. Hugo, M.D.
Robert A. Ingram, M.D.
Lucien Isräel, M.D.
David Jarovsky, Ph.D.
John B. Kethley, Ph.D.
Melvin J. Krant, M.D.
Janice R. Kuebler
Christian K. Laine
Harry W. Linde, Ph.D.
Shirley Sage Litt
Walter K. Long, M.D.
Franklin Lounsbury, M.D.
Kenneth Luurs
Alan McDermott
James L. McGee, M.D.
Carl M. Mansfield, M.D.
George (Dewey) Mead
Hugo Melvoin, Esq.
Joseph T. Michels, Jr., M.D.
Lowell F. Millburn, M.D.
Rodney R. Million, M.D.
Percy D. Mims
Cozzetta Morris
E. Michael Msall, M.D.
Jerry Myers and Dorothy
    Myers
Eleanor Nauseta
Charles F. Newlin, Esq.
Maxine Noonan
John Paxson

Jessie Potter, D.H.S.
Leonard R. Prosnitz, M.D.
The late James Quinn, III,
    M.D.
Rev. J. Wilson Reed, Jr.
Dennis Rezendes
Dorothy Rodriguez, R.N.
Gerald Rosen, M.D.
Albert L. Rubin, M.D.
Daniel K. Schlorf, Esq.
Karen Selin, M.D.
Richard Severo
Edwin S. Shneidman, Ph.D.
Tom Snyder
Susan Sontag
Michael L. Spekter, Esq.
Eric Steele, Esq., and
    Talmadge Steele
Thomas A. Stewart
Robert Stuart
David W. Taylor, Ph.D., and
    Patsy Taylor
Armand Thomas, R.Ph.
Loy Thomas
Robert G. Twycross, D.M.
Arnel Van Gelder
J. Paul Van Nevel
Robert M. Veatch, Ph.D.
Andrew C. von Eschenbach,
    M.D.
Edward Wasserman, M.D.
Eric T. Weber, M.D.
Avery Danto Weisman, M.D.
John White and Ele White
Mildred Whiteaker
Willet F. Whitmore, Jr., M.D.
Joseph Winograd, R.Ph.

I thank the following young men and women who worked part-time for me as secretary-assistants or researchers: Danielle Beauvais; Kathryn Gallien; Kevin Hochberg; Ben Jarovsky; Dena Kadish; Thomas Lukins; Pamela Mason; James Scheuermann; Kathleen Smith; William Stametz; and Alan Cohen, my current researcher.

Five friends made singular contributions to this project. I shall always be indebted to:

Sally Murakami, my talented assistant, who despite her capable background still refers to herself as my secretary and is also outstanding in that role. But I more value Sally's insights, editorial skills, sensitivity to my readers' feelings, and help in keeping me modest, at least when the vehicle is the written word. Together, Sally and I worked out many of the most difficult concepts of this book.

Mary Paul, who came initially to set up a workable book-keeping system for my grant, but stayed to handle payroll and office expenses, my personal accounts, and the hopeless intricacies and errors in hospital billing systems and insurance forms. Later, when Mary had to deal with an excruciating personal tragedy, our relationship grew into that rare form of closest friendship that comes from the sharing of sadness and grief.

Emerson Day, M.D., the first physician in an administrative role to accept me into the medical community as a serious writer. Em has not agreed with all my ideas, but he is more than willing to discuss them and test them, and thus has had a special influence on parts of this book. Like John Merrill, he has told me plainly whenever my sense of J'accuse toward doctors was unfair and has done his utmost to assure medical accuracy throughout my text.

John M. Merrill, M.D., the brilliant young medical oncologist who just happened to be assigned to me while I was a cancer patient at Northwestern Memorial Hospital. John not only extended and changed my life as a cancer patient, but taught me about cancer the disease, in its myriad forms, cancer the scourge of family relationships, and cancer as it affects physician-patient relationships. John scrutinized every chapter of this book, including revisions; surely no writer has ever been given more bountiful expertise.

C. Kevin McCabe, Esq., my neighbor and friend who both taught me new dimensions of courage and refused to accept my initial tunnel vision of cancer. Kevin, whose interests and talents are multidimensional and who developed some of the computer systems for the space shuttle, introduced me to the significance of the space age. In sharing with me the excitement of space exploration, he has given my earthbound spirit the chance to soar.

This book was supported by a one-year grant from the Rita Allen Foundation of New York, expanded into a two- and then a three-year grant. Without Moore Gates, Jr., and Milton E. Cassel's remarkable expression of faith—that I could extend my life and complete my book despite recurrent setbacks from cancer—*In the Company of Others* would never have achieved publication.

The American Cancer Society, Inc., kindly administered the Rita Allen Foundation grant.

The Field Museum of Natural History, Chicago, graciously agreed to an open-end leave of absence.

I give special thanks to my brother, Herbert Reis, whose love, support, and luminous suggestions have guided me through this and other projects.

Part 1
DISCOVERY

1.

The Sign
of the Crab

"My rage is unendurable."
A cancer patient's wife

Cancer.

Rage, fear, confusion, a feeling of impotence and exile—all are born of that single chilling word.

The problem is one of image, and the image is of wretched dying and death.

We would rather have a cardiovascular or lung disease, a disintegrative neurological disease or diabetes mellitus, kidney disease or alcoholism. Agonizing as these are—and many are far worse than cancer—they seem somehow cleaner, more acceptable. Cancer is seen as unutterably foul.

In January, 1982, it was estimated that cancer would be diagnosed in eight hundred thirty-five thousand Americans that year.[1] The figure has been rising steadily each year. Though the mortality rates for those under the age of fifty-five have decreased since 1970, we see the disease as affixed to a sentence of death. In truth, cancer comes with something worse than a death sentence: the denial of ourselves as individuals still able to manage our own affairs, direct our own lives, contribute to our households and the lives of others dependent upon us; still able to make love, give love, accept love; and more able than ever to make distinctions about what is important and what is not.

Fear and mythology lead others to view us as pariahs—"He has cancer, you know." The taut statement stands alone, as if it needs no further explanation.

He has cancer. He looks just as he did yesterday, but he has this ugly, crawling thing inside, and one of these days—sooner, not later—it'll show. Best to break from him now, before it gets worse. He is no longer one of us, poor devil.

They told me I have cancer. I don't even feel it, but here within me is this vicious, rapacious, darting, malevolent power that will grasp what it wants and take my bones, my brain, and the soft organs under my ribs and flesh. How frightened I am, how frightened and how incapacitated by my fear. Where do I turn, what do I do?

I have been through all this, I understand it, and I reject it. This fear is born of both ignorance and impotence. In the face of cancer we are like the ancients, helpless against the grinding miseries of winter, tiny figures on frozen land trembling at their powerlessness to recall the diminished sun. Like the ancients, we are petrified by that which we do not understand and cannot prevent.

I have seen the expression on a decent physician's face when he hears a pathologist's report of disseminated cancer in one of his patients. That physician is chilled by his realization that the cancer already is widespread.

I have seen terror encompass a group of people when a lecturer says, "At the present rates of incidence, one out of every four of you will at some time develop cancer."

An antitrust case in Chicago a few years ago ended in favor of the plaintiff, the federal government. When the judge announced the verdict, the defendant, a local politician, sprang to his feet and shouted, "I hope you all have *cancer*."

The news media, of which I am a member, outrages me by using obscene-sounding phrases such as "removal of the comedienne's cancerous breast," or "the senator's cancerous bladder." The image is of a body part abscessed and putrefied with cancer, though in reality the comedienne's breast harbored a malignant tumor barely two centimeters across and the tumor in the senator's bladder was scarcely larger. Why such horrendous imagery?

Nor is there justification for the phrase *cancer victim*. To be a victim is to be doomed. How strange that the media never use the word "victim" for someone who has had a heart attack—unless the corpse lies on a slab in a morgue.

I despise the term *cancer victim* because it is separatist, discriminatory, and damning; a premature farewell. I have made my feelings clear in my newspaper column, in interviews, from lecture platforms, and over network television. I think I am understood, but then I hear myself described as a cancer victim. How cruel and demeaning it is when others insist we must live with their prejudices and fears.

That is why it is so hard to admit that we have or have had cancer. With this admission we lay our acceptance as human beings on the line. And our fears are borne out by the consequences: the ineptitude and self-consciousness of others, their inanities and their stupid clichés prompted by panic. And then the final hurt—they flee.

Alas, the one who has cancer cannot flee. He has to live with his cancer as best he can. He is the one who painfully but triumphantly returns to work after surgery—only to have the personnel director pull him aside by midmorning to say: "I have to ask you not to use the drinking fountain. It's upsetting the others. I know you understand." *Understand? What is there to understand, except that the glory of return from the most fearsome precipice is suddenly dust in my mouth? The welcome earlier was not genuine but a lie. I was so proud to be back I didn't see that . . . or the fear.*

"How do you have the nerve to swim in this pool?"

"My husband left me after I had my mastectomy. He said he couldn't bear cripples."

"My wife has taken the kids and gone back to her parents. She couldn't handle my prognosis."

"Sometimes my mother's friends come to visit her, but they talk over her, not to her. If I weren't her only son, I'd bundle them out of the house. I still might."

"Our son, age twenty-four, has had Hodgkin's disease. He is fine now but is being defeated by the job market. Nobody will hire him, because of his medical history, not even for a shipping department job during the three weeks of the Christmas rush. Our son is ambitious and qualified. Do you have any solution?"

"We went back to our twenty-year duplicate bridge game after my husband recovered. Afterward, when we went into the dining room, my husband was given a plastic fork and spoon and a paper plate. My rage is unendurable."

"I've had osteosarcoma, like Senator Kennedy's son. I've graduated from college only to discover that because I'm uninsurable I'm not hireable. Maybe if my name were Kennedy I could make it, but it's not. Insurance companies won't differentiate between curable and doubtful-outcome cancers. I don't know why I fought so hard, do you?"

"Face it, Jory. The image of cancer is of a skull and crossbones on two legs."

"Is that what you see when you see me?"

"Yes. . . . I'm sorry, but you asked."

This is what cancer patients face. This is what it's like. A double bind of fear—our own and that of others. The harshness of the work world, where health and life insurance exist primarily for those who are born healthy and tend to stay healthy. The bankrupting costs of medical treatment. The social ostracism. The economic discrimination. The humiliation. The plight of being unacceptable.

So help me God, I do not know whether the race is for man to conquer cancer or to conquer his feelings about it.

This is why I, who have metastatic cancer which will ultimately kill me, decided to speak out with my column and this book. I can do nothing about the basic problem. The fact is that scientists do not yet know what causes cancer and therefore do not know how to guarantee its cure. But I can affect the social climate. I can fix responsibility. I can help bring about sanity and compassion and fair play.

In my first column, written in mid-July, 1977, I said: "I want to break down the emotional isolation cancer creates; through this column[2] we will exchange ideas and discover we are among friends . . . we will share our deepest feelings because shared feelings are better than emotions bottled up . . . we will build a network of emotional support such as has never existed."

I have not yet changed the world, but I am bringing some of us back from exile. We, our families, our friends, our colleagues, our lovers, our physicians, our nurses, our therapists and technicians, our clergy, are millions strong. Together, we can effect change.

Here, you and I are embarking on a new journey: we will examine the public and private consequences of cancer; we will dispel myths and ignorance; we will crusade for basic human rights and dignity. We will discover the most fundamental and, yes, rewarding aspects of living and dying. We will share, not just our fears, but courage, the richness of life, tenderness, and love. And we will do all this, as I wrote in my first column, using Hemingway's definition of courage; it has nothing to do with reckless bravery, but is *grace under pressure.*

2.

Sense
and Courage

"And now I'll tell you the truth:
I am also afraid."
*Joan of Arc to the Dauphin,
in Jean Anouilh's play* The Lark

I have heard appalling testimony to the ways some doctors give a diagnosis of cancer: a curt statement of fact, three cold words.

"You have cancer," one doctor said to a television producer who had no reason to suspect cancer, having come to the doctor merely for a routine checkup, "and I am late for my barber." With that, the doctor fled, leaving the television producer totally alone with the indigestible news.

Yet, even when a doctor tells us gently, we hear not a diagnosis but a verdict. Death. Something that was always off in the future is suddenly, barbarously real. Our death. The end of all we hold precious and dear. The obliteration of ourself. Shock. Horror. Disbelief. Panic. Naked fear. Fear springs into our mind like a devil, and there it resides, peering evilly around the corner whenever we are momentarily distracted.

Every disaster has its own vocabulary. One word a newly diagnosed cancer patient hears immediately from a compassionate doctor, though it slides right by at the time, is *management*. It is a medical concept, and it is an important one. "Your tumor, your kind of cancer, is one we can manage. We will do this and this and that and that. . . ." Any postoperative problems we might have can be managed. Side effects from treatment or medication can be managed. Pain can be managed. The only way I have not heard the word used by anyone in the medical profession is in connection with our unbearable emotions. Yet, as I now know, terror, fear, anger, depression, despair, grief can be softened, their stabbing points blunted, the pain they cause eased, and even overcome.

Out of our initial chaotic jumble of feelings and the recurrent, surrealist sense that this cannot be happening to us, we grope toward internal control. I am constantly awed by how adroitly so many of us manage anxieties, frustrations, fears. It is not a matter of education or sophistication. It comes from difficult lessons learned earlier, before the trauma of cancer; or when, with the advent of cancer, we suddenly understand how precarious life is and how precious.

An Iowa farmer in his seventies wrote to me several times on behalf of his wife, who has cancer. He had a farmer's deep understanding of the inevitable cycle of life, but he had no intention of giving up before he had to. Was everything that could be done for his wife being done? In the course of our correspondence he revealed an inner fiber strong as an oak, leaving no room for self-pity or moaning. I shall never forget him, or the steady way he handled his unspoken fears.

My own model at the time I struggled to accept the reality of cancer was Jean Anouilh's *The Lark*. I had seen it in New York years earlier, an adaptation by Lillian Hellman, with Julie Harris as Joan of Arc trying to shore up Charles, the weakling Dauphin of France, who was forever insisting that he was a "poor frightened nothing with a lost kingdom and a broken army." In the one scene I remembered almost verbatim, Joan offers to teach Charles "how not to be afraid," and Charles says pathetically, "I've told you the truth: I am afraid. . . .".

Joan: And now I'll tell you the truth: I am also afraid. And why not? Only the stupid are not afraid. What is the matter with you? Don't you understand that it was far more dangerous for me to get here than it is for you to build a kingdom? I've been in danger every minute of the way, and every minute of the way I was frightened. I don't want to be beaten, I don't want pain, I don't want to die. I am scared.

Charles: What do you do when you get scared?

Joan: Act as if I wasn't. It's that simple. Try it. Say to yourself, yes, I am afraid. But it's nobody else's business, so go on, go on. And you do go on.

Charles: Where do you go?

Joan: To the English, outside Orléans. And when you get there and see the cannon and the archers, and you know you are outnumbered, you will say to yourself, all right, they are stronger than I am, and that frightens me, as well it should. But I'll march right through because I had sense enough to get frightened first.

Charles: March through a stronger army? That can't be done.

Joan: Yes it can. If you have sense and courage. . . .[1]

Sense, courage, and matter-of-fact acceptance of fear—shining facets of a lodestar guiding us through the perils of life. Brilliant facets that offer focus on something grander than our pitiful selves. I followed the lodestar time and again over the years, and it was there for me when I needed to learn how to handle the intensity of metastatic cancer and the recurrent erosive feelings of having been permanently separated from the rest of the human race, fragmented, doomed. *Yes,* we have cancer, *yes,* we are terrified, we admit it, *yes,* but we *go on.* We will not crumble or perish before we must.

Sense and courage teach us how to manage our feelings, especially our fear. Common sense tells us not to give up yet, because giving up means our death. Courage helps us find the reasons not to give up—the husband or wife who desperately wants us to recover, children who need us, the parent who depends on us, the close friends whose lives are intertwined with ours, the personal goal that may still be partially or even fully achieved. Without sense and courage we will be continuously angry and mean, or chronically depressed, or a little crazy.

In my first year or more with cancer, I was alternately angry and depressed and a little bit crazy. The depression and the craziness were destroying my spontaneity, my ability to care about others. The turning point came the day I realized I no longer laughed a genuine laugh, that I was so turned inward I was destroying myself. And what was I becoming? A woman made bitter, alienated from others, by despair and fear. So I began, with the help of a psychoanalyst I had worked with earlier, to look at and deal with my despair and fear.

We need to talk about our fears. But which fears and to whom? Certainly we do not voice our deepest fears to acquaintances or business colleagues; we cannot expect people with whom we have only casual relationships to understand. Nor do we reveal our most terrible anxieties to those we love; we protect them from our panic. Hence I began writing my newspaper column, "A Time for Living," as a place for us to share our feelings within a trusting relationship, to discuss our fears and our discouragement, to learn from one another.

You and I understand the emotional risks of seeking information about that which we most dread—because what we most dread might be confirmed. Who among us dares ask his doctor: is this, my worst fear, likely to happen? Furthermore, the superstition lurks that what is spoken aloud will come true; therefore, speak not about it, for unspoken it is held at bay. And so we remain silent, like terrified rabbits.

I remember the time, early in my research, when I came across a medical description of a cancer patient with such massive bone cancer that he was utterly helpless, entirely dependent on others, even to be turned on his side in bed. Since my cancer had already begun to metastasize to bone from its primary site in soft tissue, I was horrified. Finally, I showed the description to my oncologist and asked—and it took all the courage I have—"Will this be me?"

"No, it won't." But did I feel a slight pause before he

answered? Did he lie, knowing that even the gentlest "It's possible but not likely" might undermine my will to live? Surely not, but, as he himself taught me later, he couldn't be certain. Though some cancers "behave" in somewhat orderly ways, there is no guarantee that they will. Cancer is the most unpredictable of diseases; neither we nor our physicians can ever know precisely what lies ahead. Yet, through sheer will power and determination to fight it, many of us do alter and mitigate its effect on us, and extend our lives.

I will never forget the rainswept morning I arrived a few minutes late for a postgraduate seminar on the management of common neoplasms (tumors). The seminar was my introduction to one aspect of medical education in a medical setting—in this instance, faculty members of a university medical school addressing private-practice physicians who were trying to update their knowledge of cancer.

Dripping wet, clutching umbrella, syllabus, and walking stick, I entered the handsomely appointed auditorium just as the breast cancer specialist at the podium said, "Any woman who is a bilateral mastectomee and whose cancer has metastasized is *doomed*." I have no idea what he said next. Until that moment I had not known with such utter finality that I could not beat the disease: I am a bilateral mastectomee whose cancer has metastasized.

I stood there chilled with fear, the wet umbrella dripping onto the carpet. My feet seemed nailed to the floor. The auditorium tilted toward me, the speaker seemed to be staring at me, nausea rose in my throat, and only a self-imposed don't-you-dare-vomit pulled me through. *You came here to learn,* I reminded myself. *Get into that seat and learn.*

I obeyed myself and took notes and completed the seminar, and I taught myself a little, as I must constantly, about conquering fear. I became living proof of the fact that the word *doomed,* though dramatic, and in one sense true, is in another sense one man's overstatement. For surely if we live several years or more with cancer we cannot go about continuously feeling doomed.

The sense of immediacy lessens, as it should. And if we are sensible and courageous, we recognize that we are not doomed; that at least we are in the rare position of knowing what we will die of and having time to accommodate to that knowledge.

We who have cancer need to understand what the rest of society tries to forget: that dying is simply the end of living, that "life cycle" is not a meaningless phrase. The problem is that most of us live in urban environments completely detached from the natural world, from its interlocked cycles of birth and death, ashes to ashes, dust to dust. Our children may mourn the goldfish floating belly-up in the fishbowl, but we adults, who flush the goldfish down the toilet, also fail to realize that a goldfish death is part of that same life cycle.

Today in America, we can avoid all contact with the reality of death. Most human dying now occurs in hospitals and nursing homes; few adults or children ever see it. But once we hear "cancer" and it is *our* cancer, we no longer can avoid ideas about death. They crowd in on us and terrify us. The problem is our ignorance: we do not know what dying is like and are not able to reconcile our dying with the natural cycle of life and death that still governs all life on earth.

With no prior experience to calm us, we are wide open to the most ghastly fantasies about dying. Like children, we are terrified of the unknown *it* that happens in an atmosphere of hushed voices, behind impregnable doors.

Yes, we are afraid. I wish to God we weren't, because fear, swelling into terror, becomes all-consuming. And then where are we? Wasting the time that is left, our precious time, which can be used to do so much good.

At least initially, we who have cancer envy those who die swiftly, of massive heart attacks, say. We err. Instantaneous death cheats us of any chance to prepare ourselves and those we love for the loss of us. Sudden death is cruel because it leaves so much unsaid, unfinished, unresolved. One minute, a beloved mate is laughing with us, the next minute he is dead. How bewildering, how unreal, how intolerable.

We who will have a period of time in which to die will at least not leave our mates, our families, our closest friends, in shock. Grieving, yes. Lonely, yes. Exhausted by the vigil, yes. But also aware that the slow transition from life to death allowed time for the deepest, most tender feelings of closeness to reinforce the lifetime shared together.

With cancer, there is almost always time, time to say what needs to be said, to do what needs to be done. To leave, through letters for the future—say, to one's family for the first Christmas without us, or to a lover, or to children for their birthdays—our dreams and hopes and wishes for them, our tenderest thoughts, our strengths, and our love.

There *is* an advantage to knowing what we are likely to die of. Time can work for us as well as against us. Time given, because of cancer, allows us to share memories of the best of our times together and the sadness of having to say good-bye. With cancer, we rarely leave those we love stunned, as others are, when death comes without warning.

If we are open and sensible about our dying, we can give immeasurable strength to ourselves and those we love most dearly. When we are armed with such courage, our fear of death recedes.

3.

Anger
as Freedom

"Do not go gentle into that good night,
Rage, rage against the dying of the light."
Dylan Thomas

Anger is as basic to cancer as fear. It is a normal response to sudden, wrenching, irrevocable change that shatters all our expectations, our plans, and our sense of future.

Even if frustration or bitter disappointment has characterized our lives, most of us will discover that a diagnosis of cancer changes our perspective 180 degrees. Now life is precious, and God, O God, we don't want it taken from us, now or ever.

The unrecognized calamity of cancer is not that we may die of it, but that we are so likely to lose our autonomy to it. From the time our doctor, or a surgeon we've just met, says, "I want you in the hospital on Wednesday," we are expected to behave like patients, quietly acquiescing in the doctor's, the medical team's, and the hospital's rules. Beginning in the hospital admissions office, the message is clear: "The little plastic band [placed] on the arm of the patient as part of the admitting process [is] an expression of property rights. . . . It means we now take possession of you."[1]

Hospitals exist to heal people, but in order to be treated in a hospital every patient must fit into a preexisting slot. Strangers take over: doctors, nurses, aides, technicians, orderlies—mainly cool and self-distancing personnel, oblivious to the depersonalizing effect they have on us. In a teaching hospital with a cancer center, teams of specialists, medical students, and a full house staff (interns and residents) take even fuller control of our bodies and our lives. We are expected to be part of the team, but only in a passive, compliant role.

To hospital personnel, our fear, our insecurity, our overwhelming feeling of having received a death-sentence, are commonplace. House staff and nurses *expect* cancer patients to be frightened and anxious, but all too often their understanding of fear and anxiety is superficial. They do not, or cannot, allow themselves to feel what we now feel: the nausea and terror of having been abruptly torn loose from our moorings to confront the world's most feared disease.

So, except for the impersonal touch of physical examination, or a change of dressings, we are like untouchables to the hospital personnel. In their own eyes, they are correctly professional. They signal they want no involvement. The message, alas, comes when we are most vulnerable, most in need of expressions of love and concern.

We resent the arbitrary obliteration of self, but because we are weak and, perhaps, in postsurgical pain, we are rarely able to voice our feelings. I remember only a few occasions when I could use my anger to effect change. One was during a bone scan, a long procedure in which a patient, semiconfined by sandbags, had to lie motionless under a heavy metal scanner which passed with paleolithic slowness over his body and then back again and yet again.[2] This enormous disklike piece of equipment was less than an inch above one's nose and, because it moved so slowly, most patients were asked if they suffered from claustrophobia. If the answer was yes, as mine was, the technician monitoring the scan usually sat near enough that the patient could feel his presence, and usually offered reassuring comments during the scan. Conversation between patient and technician was not permitted, because talking created head motion.

On this particular occasion, I was wretchedly nauseated and in considerable pain. Lying flat on my back, motionless, for the necessary twenty-three minutes was close to unbearable. The technician, a young man, disappeared as soon as he knew the scanner was functioning properly; a young woman I assumed was another technician seated herself somewhere out of my sight and proceeded to rattle through a newspaper.

My claustrophobia mounted. My pain was intense. Her lack of concern infuriated me. I yearned to knock the newspaper out of her hands and yell, "Pay attention to me, *pay attention.*" Instead, I had to use most of those twenty-three minutes to convince myself that I was not going to suffocate. The balance of the time I spent wondering how to use the experience to help patients who would come after me.

When the scan ended, I swallowed my anger and asked the young woman how long she'd been working in the department. She was a technician in training; this was her second week. "You know," I said, "you could do more for your patients and also make the job rewarding for yourself."

"I could?"

"Yes, you could. Try that scanner on a dry run with yourself as the patient. Learn how frightening it is to lie under it. Lie there immobile, silent, scared, alone. I felt alone because you buried yourself in your newspaper. I needed some concern from you. That would have been comforting. You are part of the healing process, you know."

A small thing, but I got through to her. Later I even laughed at Jory Graham, crusader for cancer patients, who on this occasion thought she had scored a tiny victory.

This incident occurred during my third year as a cancer patient. By then I had been hospitalized seven or eight times and was no stranger to the department of radiation therapy, or to diagnostic radiology, or to nuclear medicine (where I reported for scans). I was no longer intimidated by the hospital system, and I felt entitled to speak out. Yet from the start I was outraged by it, because it forces patients to initiate overtures of friendship to medical personnel at the time they feel least capable of reaching out.

I wanted that student-technician to understand how much good she could do by reaching out; I wanted everyone in the hospital system to understand and acknowledge by word and gesture the human needs of cancer patients. I saw the unnecessary frustration and despair brought into play each time the system ignored those needs. Patients must have something with which to build hope; optimism ("You must be optimistic," say the doctors) cannot replace feelings of depression and defeat easily, if at all.

The inhospitality of hospitals is felt by many patients. But those with a fractured bone, a hernia, or a painful gallbladder have enormous advantages. For one thing, they know their pain will subside and vanish as their bodies heal. For another, they know they will soon return to the normal routines of their lives. They may rail at the hospital system, but they can tolerate it, because their stay is relatively short and almost without fear.

A hospitalized cancer patient has none of these securities. Hospitalization alone does not ensure healing and in many instances it marks another setback. For a cancer patient, it is often an ordeal beyond the comprehension of his physician, the house staff, his family, and his friends. He cannot talk about it to any of them, because, in one way or another, all these people have demonstrated that they do not want to listen to minute details of feelings he can only timidly express. Further, they are trying so hard to reassure him, and so much of the reassurance sounds false, that he feels conned and even more insecure. Are they withholding information about his illness? Are they making decisions for him on the basis of their greater knowledge of his condition? What do they know that he isn't being told? What does his doctor mean when he says, "You must be optimistic"? How can anyone feel optimism in the face of what is clearly another battle lost to cancer? The cancer patient is too weak to protest, yet his perceptions are often as keen as his pain, and just as stabbing.

As hospitalized cancer patients, we understand that we are

objects of medical care. Once discharged, we often discover we have become objects in our own world, too, where we are now seen as "the terminally ill," or as another "cancer victim." People who sent flowers and get-well cards to us in the hospital now feel they have exhausted these conventional forms of showing concern. Our homecoming removes the distance between us and they feel uneasy with the new closeness. The comfortable relationships we shared before give way to timidity and awkwardness. How quickly we come to know the signals of their instant need to retreat. And though we feel like pleading, "Stay, stay, I've come back from the brink and I'm weak and I'm weary and lonely and I need you," we have pride, and dignity, and a much greater understanding of their feelings than they have of ours, and so we are tactful and let them go.

What is harder to release, because there is no outlet for it, is our anger at their illogical fears, at their need to flee. *Dammit, don't you understand where I've been, what I've come through, what a triumph it is to be alive? Can't you understand how I hurt and how you are adding to the hurt? I didn't ask to have cancer, I didn't go looking for it; despite what has happened to me I'm still me. Come back. There's nothing to fear. You can't catch what I've got. It's not your life that's at stake. You're not trapped—I am. You're free to continue your life just as it is. You're so blessedly free.*

Oh, if only we could be free again, free of the hateful disease and the fear and anger and despair that it brings, over and over again. We nearly strangle on emotions; together, they create untold suffering and demoralization. So we turn to God, the last resort for many of us who have been remote from God since childhood. And all of us ask God one question: Why me?

Why me, and not that bum down the block who beats his wife and terrifies his kids? Why me, and not that power-drunk vice president who heads my department? Why me, just on the edge of achievement, rather than the crazed old woman who fishes about in the garbage cans along the alley for the discards of our meals? Why me, and not the really evil people in this world?

Who sent this gnawing worm into me, You or the devil? What am I—a sinner? All right, I'm a sinner. I was impatient with my mother

*when her brain began to dull. Yes, and angry with her for becoming
senile and incompetent. I despised my weak father. I've belittled my
wife—and cheated on her. But to get cancer for these, the acts of men
everywhere?*

We fumble through a Bible. *Here it is, here in St. John it says,
"If ye shall ask anything in my name, I will do it." Do it. Cure me.
I ask You. I beg You. And tell me, why me?*

In July, 1977, I wrote "Coming to Terms with 'Why Me?' " It
was my third column for the *Chicago Daily News,* the first U.S.
newspaper to run my column. I wrote it during the week I was
moving from an apartment I loved. It was in a building that had
turned condominium, and in the face of cancer, I could not afford
to buy it. My father refused to lend what I would have needed to
make the down payment. He thought it was insane to buy real
estate when you were doomed. I was tired and ill at the time
because of all the radiation I had been receiving, and moving was
a nightmare. I tried lifting something and felt as if the vertebrae in
my lumbar spine had collapsed. Pain was instant and excruciating.
I had to go for emergency examinations and x-rays. I was lucky:
no bone had compressed and fractured. But I was incapable of
pain-free motion, and the only release was to lie on the floor and
let its hardness mitigate the awful pain.

Lying on the floor, surrounded by packing cases and the
disorder of moving, I worked with my tape recorder and drafted
"Coming to Terms with 'Why Me?' "

"The question is pitiful, unavoidable, and normal," I told my
readers. I had asked it of myself when I first learned I had
cancer—and needed months to forge an answer.

An answer; there is no *one* answer. Each of us has to come to
terms with *why me?* in our own way. However, I outlined four
possible answers.

The first answer to *why me?* originates in Genesis: God has
selected this illness for me because of my sin; I am being
punished.

A second answer is a late twentieth-century form of paranoia:
Society is doing this to me. It's our tense, pressured environment.
Everything is polluted. Everything is contaminated.

A third answer to *why me?* is a pseudopsychological notion: I have brought this on myself. I'm a failure as a human being and driven by unconscious needs to seek a way out.

A fourth answer is existentialist: The universe is absurd. The tragedies that befall us are a matter of luck. Luck is random. This just happened to catch me.

These are the major choices, and I personally find all but the last of them categorically untrue. To believe that cancer has been aimed at us by a vengeful God is to further burden ourselves with unnecessary guilt. If we are all sinners, how can some of us be selected to suffer while others go free?

Blaming society is simply an extension of a lifetime of blaming everyone else for one's own problems. A paranoid answer is no answer at all.

The idea that we bring about our own disease strikes me as the wildest theorizing from knowledge of psychosomatic medicine. To state that some of us have cancer-prone personalities is not only a cruel accusation but a stupid one. How do these researchers explain cancer in newborn infants? How developed can a cancer-prone personality be at birth?

Fortunately, for every psychologist who insists upon associating a cell disease like cancer with certain adult personality traits, there is a psychiatrist or psychoanalyst who will say, "I wish the notion were true. If it were, we could cure you."

A friend whose young wife died of cancer told me that she had tortured herself wondering if she were responsible for her condition. "She was depressed enough just dealing with the cancer," he said, "without having to feel she had brought it on herself. That simply exacerbated her problems, and the worst of it was, it was so unproven and untrue."

Which brings us to existentialism. I opt for it because it offers hope and also because I believe that our ordered universe is, in many ways, absurd. The way to find meaning in an absurd situation is to take some kind of action. My action was a search for a different perspective on *why me?*, because the question is so loaded with implications of injustice. Since I could not blame God, or myself, or the polluters of our environment, I was confounded—and angry. I didn't know why I had cancer (I still don't), but the unfairness of losing my freedom and my life to it filled me with rage.

One day, though, I tried finding an answer with that old puzzle that presents three rows of three dots each, as follows:

Without retracing your path, you are to draw four connecting lines that pass through every dot. The problem is *not* solved by drawing a box, like the one below, because this takes five lines.

The solution depends on your ability to think *outside the box.*

I was tinkering with the solution because I only half recalled it, but my mind was on *why me?* Suddenly it occurred to me to think outside the question, that is, turn the question around and ask, why *not* me? My mind opened instantly.

Why not me? Who am I to be so special that I cannot get cancer? Who am I to be so egocentric as to believe that random luck is for others, but not me? From then on, it was only a matter of time to *it is me,* and, *what am I going to do now?* With this question came a feeling of enlightenment and a sense of power.

We cease feeling trapped and powerless once we recognize

that we can still make decisions and have choices. The choices may be radically limited by the extent of our illness, and the decisions may often seem meager, but knowing we have them to make can alleviate some of our sense of powerlessness. This is true for those of us who were heavy smokers and have cancer of the lung or larynx; and for those of us who continued to work in asbestos plants long after we clearly understood the carcinogenic dangers there. We may feel we're being punished, but the truth is that smoking, or remaining in the asbestos plant, was an action we chose freely. The risk was a risk we were willing to take. We gambled. We lost.

Do we now destroy all meaning and any pleasure in the time that is left by wallowing in self-hatred? No, we do not. We need to use our decision-making ability to help our families and friends through the ordeal that lies ahead. That's what we still can do, and that's what matters now.

I made the decision to use the rest of my life on behalf of cancer patients everywhere. Along with many of my readers, I also decided that no hour alone or with those I love would be wasted in self-pity or guilt. I said to my readers, we simply have no time to waste. The time we do have is for reaching out, giving, building our own legacy of courage and concern for others.

If we are not to sink into chronic depression and helpless anger, we have to go beyond the futile attempt to find an answer to *why me?* to acceptance of the fact that we have cancer: *I have it. Now what do I do?* This is the decision that will give meaning and significance to the rest of our life, despite physical limitations, recurrent frustration, and fear.

In accepting cancer as the probable cause of my death, I realize that I now have nothing but my life to lose. I am free to speak out, to crusade for the rights of cancer patients everywhere. The fact that I have a column means only that I have a wider audience to reach. Yet my voice is nothing if it is not joined by yours.

The image of a cancer patient retreating from the mainstream is often accurate. Sometimes an individual is pressured into retreat by the discrimination he encounters. Other times, he is so ashamed of having cancer, or so terrified of it, that he creates a wall of silence to hide behind.

I do not accept the image of retreat, and I do not let others dictate the confines on my life. One theme that runs through my newspaper column like a *leitmotif* is the belief that we should not give up before we must; that by our actions, by our behavior inside and outside the hospital, we will change the image of the demoralized, pitiful cancer patient. The dialogue between my readers and me in "A Time for Living" shows repeatedly the courage and determination characteristic of most of the cancer patients I know. The column reinforces their inner strength, their rejection of the cruel attitudes of others, and their affirmation that anger in these situations is justified and can be put to work for us.

I once wrote a strong letter to a man who'd been a close friend but who could not deal with my cancer. I told him to get off his duff and get back to me. Though my letter failed to bring him back, it served another purpose: in writing it, I realized I was not so helpless after all.

I have written more than one column on the meanness inherent in the label "cancer victims,"[3] that odious label used daily by all the media and even by the American Cancer Society. Some members of the media and the ACS are beginning to understand the need for change.

Angered over the ostracism he encountered as a cancer patient, Orville Kelly, a small-town Iowa newspaper editor, founded Make Today Count, a support group, in 1974. Kelly's purpose was, "to allow cancer patients and their families an opportunity to come together and discuss their emotional problems." It's not surprising that more than 270 Make Today Count groups are currently active in the United States and other countries.

Equally angry because of the ways the human needs and fundamental human rights of cancer patients are being ignored, I joined with approximately thirty-five caring physicians, lawyers, business men and women, and cancer patients and their families. In 1979, we founded a new issue-oriented national organization: One/Fourth, The Alliance For Cancer Patients And Their Families.[4]

Because almost nobody knows how to handle anger, cancer patients are expected to suppress their anger about the way the disease is destroying their lives. That is unrealistic and unhealthy. Suppressing anger is not the answer—it too often leads to chronic depression and shortened life span[5]—yet the function of healthy expressions of anger is not understood at all.

I was furious when my cancer metastasized and nailed me onto the endangered list. I'd fought hard to win the first round, yet seven months later I had to enter the match again and make an even greater effort, though with little hope of winning more than added time. I was so frustrated, so disappointed, so thwarted because the earlier effort seemed to have been in vain that I lashed out at everyone—and all but drove them away.

Fear that they might not return brought me to my senses. After all, they were not to blame for my disease, and it was unfair to ask them to listen to a long-playing diatribe. I began looking for creative ways to handle anger. I asked my readers to contribute their solutions. My favorite answers are these, from two readers who have become good friends of mine:

Patty Grate wrote that she made a rag bag the size of a Santa Claus pack. When she becomes so angry that she feels she's "going to kill," she hauls the rag bag into the bathroom and closes the door and the cover to the toilet. "And then I sit on the convenience and tear rags into shreds until the utter stupidity of what I am doing gets to me and I can come out laughing again."

Michael Spekter wrote that he was going to have fourteen-by-sixteen enlargements made of his pathology slides. "I'll mount them as dart boards and hurl darts at the dark areas that show tumors."

A doctor finally suggested to me that I learn to shout, "I hate having cancer." I felt silly and self-conscious the first few times I tried, but I learned to say it to empathetic friends. In a funny way it helps, because it's an honest statement. It does not drive away friends, because it does not blame them for our misfortune. It is a legitimate focus for our very real anger, anger that threatens to get out of hand but is diffused by a simple statement of fact.

Healthy anger gives us vitality. It is a glorious sign that we're far from dead. It makes us fight for our jobs—and pride makes us work twice as hard at them. Healthy anger gives us purpose, challenges us to make new decisions, encourages old ideas: to enroll in the courses we've always wanted to take; to embark on the trip we've always wanted to make; to create the journal that is our legacy to our children and our grandchildren . . .

"Do not go gentle into that good night,
Rage, rage against the dying of the light."[6]

Part 2
PHYSICIANS AND PATIENTS: HUMAN DIGNITY AND RIGHTS

4.

A Patient's Right to Know

"When truth is gone, everything is
gone. . . ."
*A nurse who lied to countless cancer patients
about their diagnoses and then learned she
herself had pancreatic cancer*

A surgeon, clean of blood but still in his operating-room fatigues,
enters the lounge beyond the hospital recovery room to confer
with the anxious family of the patient on whom he has just
performed surgery. The lounge is crowded, but surgeon and
family manage to form a tight little private group. "How is he?"
they ask. "What did you find?"

The surgeon says, "He's doing fine, but I am sorry to say we
found a malignancy."

The family, which has been waiting nervously since the
surgery was first scheduled, gasps and feels as if it has been dealt a
death blow. Though they have feared the possibility of cancer,
they never discussed their fears, but swallowed them individually
and prayed they would not be realized. Now, with devastating
clarity, they understand that tragedy has struck all of them, not
simply the one who has the disease. As their horror mounts, a
protective question forms, and they ask the surgeon, "Do we have
to tell him?"

Now the surgeon's dedication is to healing and cure; these

are the reasons he chose medicine as his profession in the first place. Every cancer case stirs old anxieties that began in medical school: Will I be competent and effective? *With cancer, I am frustrated in my professional role; with cancer, I fail. Failure is intolerable. Turn from it. Flee. Let the family handle this; they've offered.* Damn, he wishes it were otherwise, but he has done the best he can.

Thus, doctor and family make a decision that will prove more disastrous than the disease itself. They will "spare" the human being who has cancer his bad news.

The truth is, they spare no one except the surgeon, who is not the family physician but a stranger called upon to confirm the diagnosis and to perform the surgery.

Sooner or later, every cancer patient knows he has the disease. Generally, he knows almost from the moment his brain begins to clear itself from the fog of anesthesia. Suspecting cancer for weeks or months before he ever saw a doctor, he frames a question to the nurse who is attending him in the recovery room: "What did they find?" Instead of stating what "they found," the nurse hushes him with an overly cheerful comment about how good it is that he's now awake enough to be returned to his room.

Transferred from the hospital cart to his bed, hooked to his I.V., he opens his eyes to see his family. They smile, but they aren't dancing about in glee at the end of his bed because the never-discussed but feared malignancy turned out to be something else. They are somber, ill at ease, and they evade his mumbled questions with murmurs: "Try to sleep. . . . Don't worry about anything. . . ."

Alone with the night nurse who comes in with a fresh I.V., he is more alert and he tries again: "What did they find?" Her code of ethics prevents her from revealing the diagnosis, so her answer is hasty and inept: "You'll have to ask your doctor."[1]

Thus he learns that what he most feared is true.

But worse than his knowledge of his cancer is the implicit meaning of the evasions: that he is doomed. Now he understands why no one is open and honest. It is not because he has cancer but because he is going to die of it shortly; his doctor and his family are too shocked to admit such devastating news.[2] He wants desperately to talk to them, comfort them, be comforted by them; he needs to shout and yell his terror and hear words of affection and love that will let him know they share his anguish and will stand by him and help him through the perilous journey to his death. Two lines from the Navy Hymn[3] echo endlessly in his brain: "Oh, hear us when we cry to thee / For those in peril on the sea." He is in peril, he is drowning in horror and fear. And no one will hear him, though he urgently needs to be heard.

Plunged into anguish, he accepts the lie his doctor tells him the next morning; he is mute, isolated, condemned, and utterly without hope.

In the autumn of 1977, Ronald Kotulak, science writer for the *Chicago Tribune*, reported the following heartbreaking story under the headline "Children and Death: No More Pretending"[4]:

> For three years Lisa's parents did everything they could to prevent their young daughter from learning she was dying of leukemia. They told her instead that she had anemia.
>
> When the 12-year-old died . . . her parents were heartbroken but they were consoled somewhat because they thought Lisa had been spared the agony of knowing she had deadly . . . cancer during her three-year illness.
>
> But Lisa did know, right from the beginning. While going through the child's belongings, her mother came across Lisa's diary in which she kept a careful account of her diagnosis, medications, and blood counts.
>
> Her mother sat down and cried. All those years of lying and pretending had been wasted. Instead of sharing one of life's deepest tragedies, they had played a game of pretend.
>
> "Lisa ended up sharing her worries and concerns with her diary because she didn't want to upset her parents by letting them know she knew she was dying," said Dr. Helen Maurer, a pediatrician and blood specialist at Children's Memorial Hospital. . . . "In the past, when we tried to conceal the truth, that was often more frightening to the children than the reality of their death."

Denial and refusal of the right to talk about one's own life-threatening disease is the ultimate cruelty. It is solitary confinement, as bleak and unremitting as in any prison where, you realize, it is used as punishment for wrongdoing. Though in this instance the motive is entirely different, the effect of a family's and physician's refusal to admit cancer is identical. The person who knows he has the disease but is not permitted to talk about it is locked behind a monumental wall of silence, with no way to escape to the safe haven of loving arms that will comfort and hold close. No one should ever be condemned to such total isolation. No rationalization exists to support such punishment.

I understand how families blunder into this tragedy. The leaden news of cancer blots out any ability to look ahead to the consequences of the initial lie. No family can anticipate all the lies that will subsequently need to be invented to support the first lie. Or even the immediate need to post a family member as sentinel outside the patient's room in order to tell everyone entering what to say: all the physicians and medical students who will see the patient, all the nurses on the hospital's three shifts, all the hospital aides and technicians, and the children, the relatives, and closest friends. (Will the family lie to them or tell the truth?)

Families simply do not understand the skills needed to be actors twenty-four hours a day for an unknown length of time that can stretch into years. Even if they are trained actors, the constant monitoring will drain them of their own vitality. Home, the one place that can be a haven, becomes a guarded camp of caution where even watching television is feared—someone might be interviewing a cancer patient with identical symptoms and treatment. What if their dear one puts two and two together?

But worse than the exhausting burden they create for themselves is their unwitting declaration of instant incompetence on the part of the one who has cancer. Before surgery, that individual was fully accepted in his role as the breadwinner and head of the household, or the grandparent who not only raised a family but pulled through the catastrophe of the Depression and a World War, or the emerging adolescent in search of his identity, his right to make decisions about himself. Regardless of age or sex, the family member who has cancer is no less competent now than he was before the verification of his disease. That notion is a family and a societal misconception born of the demoralizing mythology of cancer, not reality.

We respect physicians because we believe they have dedicated their lives to the relief of suffering. We believe they are ethical and moral, and we expect them to be kindly and have our best interests at heart. Even if we do not know the law, we understand that the basic patient-physician relationship is a one-to-one relationship in which confidentiality is paramount. Thus, we are shocked when doctors are willing to accommodate a lie, especially one that betrays the trust we brought to our relationship with them.

We find unacceptable the rationalizations physicians offer for failures to be truthful with their patients. Their shabby excuses reflect a lack of confidence in our ability to define our own courage and direct our own lives, and reflect as well their own "phobia of death"[5]:

"I am just old-fashioned enough to believe that a patient's family knows best."

"His wife told me that he's always said he'd commit suicide if he developed cancer. I can't be responsible for that."

"I don't believe this patient can handle the information."

Like all rationalizations, these are flawed. The statement about suicide is wildly imprecise. Suicide statistics simply do not bear out the notion of thousands of newly diagnosed cancer patients annually jumping off bridges, putting guns to their heads, or swallowing lethal doses of pills. If a doctor were interested in finding supporting data on suicide, he would have long ago checked with the National Cancer Institute. NCI, established in 1938, treats some sixty thousand patients yearly. Dr. Vincent DeVita, Jr., its director, who conducted his own investigation, found that NCI has a record to date of exactly two suicides. One of these was an NCI staff physician who did not have cancer; the other, a cancer patient who was well on the road to recovery, but who, ironically, did not know how far ahead she was.

In the first and third instances above, the physician is

frequently a surgeon who has seen the patient only once before performing the surgery. This surgeon cannot possibly "know" the patient or the patient-family relationship. He has no way of knowing whether the patient is the one strong person to whom the others have always turned, or whether the family is at odds with itself and badly fragmented. It is a myth that all cancer patients have loving families eager to help them make a come-back. Many do not.

The matter of a patient's ability to "handle" bad news is also based on a physician's judgment. Legally, this judgment is called "therapeutic privilege," and until the mid-1970s "therapeutic privilege" was upheld in court cases. But the climate has changed. Civil-rights laws, like ideas about feminism, have not merely accumulated; they have changed and strengthened our fundamen-tal ideas about self-determination. In contemporary America, we believe we can effect societal change. We have seen, and perhaps are active participants in, movements for change. But even if we have never walked in a civil-rights or anti–nuclear energy march, we have become part of the common struggle for egalitarianism. The spectacle of a President who believed he had the privilege of lying to us produced more than shock. Watergate revolted us because it mocked our common belief that we have a fundamental right to know the truth.

So, as Professor Robert Veatch[6] notes, the "therapeutic priv-ilege argument has fallen upon hard times. . . . Challenges have in-creased among lawyers, philosophers, and even physicians. . . ."[7]

Unless we are incompetents in the legal sense of the word, we have grown up believing we will control our destinies. All of us, from early childhood on, test our independence in various ways.[8] The right to make decisions about our futures is taken for granted in this country, which still trumpets the small-town origins of those Presidents who came from simple families. The triumphant theme, "every boy can grow up to become President," dies slowly, even among those of us who realize that money and organized power and television campaigns are now integral to the ascent to the White House.

Still, we do know we control ourselves. We choose to be

moral or immoral, kindly or cruel, open- or closed-minded, friendly or aloof. We decide how important fairness and integrity are to us. We create our image of the person we want to be, and, mainly, we endeavor to live up to that image. When a disease like cancer is found within our bodies, part of the shock and horror of the revelation is our sense of wrongness that this should happen to us.

Sympathetic but uncomprehending feature writers who interview cancer patients are wont to use the dramatic phrase, "Betrayed by his body, he . . ." But the real betrayal is a conspiracy between family and physician to withhold the admission of our cancer, for that is a betrayal of trust, of our confidence that those who care about us will be honest with us. "When truth is gone, everything is gone," the nurse mourned, and she died despising herself for the amends she could never make.

Each bundle of reader mail generated by my column includes letters from families who thought that by lying they were doing the "right thing." They write to me long after the funeral, when the full impact of the relationship they destroyed hits. They hope for comfort, hope I will know how to assuage their bitter, self-denunciating grief. Now, when death has indeed parted them from a loved parent or spouse or child, they understand the tragedy they created. They robbed themselves and the one who is dead of the comfort and unity that could have been achieved, cheated everyone out of closeness and sharing of grief, and denied everyone the right to say what needed to be said—"I love you; I will miss you; I want to thank you for all the joy you gave me."

I read these admissions with sorrow because the error cannot be undone. Loss compounded by guilt is a dreadful burden that may never be resolved.

As a cancer patient who has been lied to (for me it was the prognosis, not the diagnosis), I know the tremendous hurt and anger that come when truth is finally revealed. I would have lived at least one year of my life differently, but that year, taken from me by physicians, is irretrievable. So is my confidence in them. I took my inconsolable feelings of loss and injustice and fled, with no wish to see those physicians again. One of them was my father, who subsequently developed lung cancer and died of it, locked into denial of his own death. There was no way to breach the chasm he had created. Inadmission of his own mortality was his choice.

If we choose to deny an illness because that is the only way to accommodate to it, that is also our privilege, though I would add that refusal to discuss it creates a whole different set of problems for the families that are involved. These families write to me constantly, asking for guidance, but I am never entirely certain that my suggestions will be helpful. I can offer only some possible reasons for the close-mouthed stoicism of the family member who has cancer, and hope these explanations will make the situation a little easier to accept.

Dr. Elisabeth Kübler-Ross, who popularized the erroneous idea that people die in stages,[9] taught that Stage I of the dying process was denial and isolation,[10] and emphasized denial to her students in a way I do not understand. I remember one of her students (a therapist) showing me a film of an interview with a dying patient. Suddenly she leaned forward and said, "Watch, watch his denial." I was shocked. Why should therapists be so hell-bent on pinning down examples of denial? That seemed unnecessarily pejorative to me. Furthermore, if one stresses denial, it becomes exceedingly difficult to understand that for some individuals denial has a far more positive quality: hope.

Hope is essential. Without it, people will indeed give up and die. Most doctors understand this; their problem is more in not knowing how to create and sustain hope. Thus, Dr. Nathan Schnaper writes that hope is as necessary to some people as "the narcotics they need for pain. . . . hope is realistic, too, since no one can predict when a patient will die. Patients constantly outlive predictions about the amount of time they have left, and in some cases have been known to outlive their doctors as well."[11]

In the Declaration of Geneva, adopted by the general assembly of the World Medical Association at Geneva, Switzerland, in September, 1948, a short list of pledges is set forth for medical students "at the time of being admitted as members of the medical profession." The fourth pledge is "I will practice my profession with conscience and dignity." I would ask medical students, who are our greatest hope for change, to answer these questions:

Where is conscience in a lie which prevents another human being from knowing what is wrong with his own body?

Where is conscience when a doctor, for whatever reason, determines that he will not reveal to his patient the most important secret in that patient's life?[12]

Where is conscience when, by entering into a cabal with a patient's family, a doctor wipes out his patient's autonomy?

Where are medical ethics when, by withholding or limiting truth (for example, "We found a few malignant cells"), a doctor so alters reality for both patient and the patient's family that they are utterly confused?

Where is your professional integrity if you, as a doctor, destroy the ancient bridge of confidence and trust?

When truth is gone, everything is gone.

In every survey that asks healthy individuals whether they would or would not want to know if they have an incurable disease, ninety percent say, yes, they want to be told. In surveys of the early 1960s that asked physicians whether or not they told, ninety percent said they did *not*—almost an exact inversion of the number of lay people who said they would want to know. This percentage has dropped in recent years, especially among medical students and recent graduates. The problem is among older physicians. The best many can say is that they "frequently disclose." But either this answer reveals a gap in the credibility of recent physician surveys, or the word "frequently" is open to interpretation, for we know that too many patients are still in the dark about their actual diagnoses. Just ask any nurse working on an internal-medicine floor.

My reader mail, which, to a large extent, consists of letters from cancer patients and their families, also shows that ninety percent of those who have the disease wanted to know both diagnosis and prognosis. About six percent of my readers are vehement about not wanting to know. The remainder give a qualified yes, they want to know, but would like to be told with compassion and gentleness. As one elderly cancer patient wrote, "I don't want bad news just *thrown* at me. Discreetly and with concern is better."

In the article I quoted above, Dr. Nathan Schnaper also gives us the following example of a physician's ineptness in discussing a diagnosis of cancer with his patients: ". . . a surgeon . . . believed that patients should be told, quite directly, and trained his residents in this approach. He later developed a carcinoma in the area of his subspecialty [sic] and his own surgeon, who was one of his former residents, being very well trained, told him 'the facts.' 'Dr. W., you have a carcinoma of . . . *and this is it.* You had better make your arrangements.' Dr. W. remained in the hospital for a year and almost every day . . . tried to have the former resident thrown off the staff."[13] [Emphasis added.]

I submit that Dr. W.'s reaction was not to the news of the cancer but to the ungentle, merciless pronouncement, "this is it." Not too long ago, I was rehospitalized because my disease was once again out of control. Everyone knew who I was, and several young doctors on the house staff who had heard me speak when they were medical students went out of their way to spend time with me. Inadvertently, one of them almost destroyed me. I had been talking at length with him about dying (it was very much on my mind at the time), and I said my fears had just been allayed by the chairman of the department of radiation therapy who had examined me and who said, "You are not dying. Your cancer is still confined to bone, and though it is causing you great pain now, that will diminish with treatment, and you will not die so long as it stays in bone."

The young doctor said, "But you and I know you are going to die of the disease." I have never felt more undermined.

I spent hours trying to understand why his words seemed so destructive, until I remembered Dr. W.'s surgeon, who said, "this is it." The two statements were identical in their unfeeling bluntness, and each conveyed a sense of finality.

When I next saw the young doctor, I told him how he had shaken me, and why. "You know," I said, "none of us wants to hear a prediction of our certain death. That's like having you write NMTBD [Nothing More To Be Done] on our chart and then rubbing our nose in it. You can't do that to a patient, ever."

Propelled by their own unconscious fear of death, many doctors agonize over how to tell a terminally ill patient he is dying. The fact is, nobody needs to tell. If a dying patient asks, "I'm dying, aren't I?" it is because he seeks medical confirmation of that which he already knows but which his family cannot accept.

"I'm dying, aren't I?" also asks for special reassurance, for those words with which a doctor admits his own sadness in facing his patient's impending loss of life: "How I wish it were otherwise. How I wish we were not coming to the time when we will need to say good-bye."

In the mid-1970s, students at medical schools across the country simultaneously discovered their need to explore medical ethics in depth and began organizing their own extracurricular ethics seminars to meet that need. By the end of the decade, formal ethics courses offered as electives were standard at many medical schools. Interest in ethics is integral to a physician's knowledge of his moral obligation to his patients. This is why medical literature for the last few years has been liberally sprinkled with articles on "how to tell," and "when to tell."[14]

I believe I have read most if not all of this literature. So it's fair to say that the journal articles inevitably fail in one respect: they never give specific examples of how to tell a diagnosis of cancer gently. The authors, primarily physicians, are sensitive to the need for gentleness but unsure of ways to convey it.

Gentleness is compassion. It is knowing that when a patient hears "cancer" and what you, his doctor, plan to do about it, his world flips upside-down, and his stomach churns. Yet at the same time, if he sees unmistakable signs of caring, he knows that with you he is as safe and secure as anyone can be under the circumstances.

Medical education needs to teach humaneness, not how to maintain a cool facade in the face of adversity. Medical education ought to give students the chance to ask patients who know they have cancer, "How were you told? How would you have preferred to hear?" Medical education is remiss in omitting the voice of the patient. It assumes a huge responsibility in speaking *for* the patient, and it too often presumes it speaks accurately.

If Dr. W. had known that "this is it" drove a stake through his patients' hearts, he would never have trained his residents to use the phrase. The bitter irony of his own diagnosis was that he recognized his brutal impact only when he became a patient. We respect his ethics, his insistence on being honest with his patients, but ache over his fear of being human and allowing his humanity to show.

With a life-threatening disease, the problem is never how to tell a dying person he is dying, but rather how to reassure even those patients who have poor prognoses that they are not dying now. Physicians who see poor prognoses are torn between their sense of horror—they feel obliged to tell such patients to "put their affairs in order"—and the normal wish not to be the one who pronounces the death-sentence.

But this dilemma is mainly specious. It is based on the presumption that nothing can be done. Oncology as a specialty is far enough ahead to say that there is virtually always something that can be done. For example: though cancer that metastasizes to the liver is still a fatal cancer, treatment now extends the lives of those who have it by a year or two. I am talking about worthwhile living and *wanted* life, not a long wasting-away. And if the patient as well as the doctor is fighting for his life, together they will extend life. This is one more reason why a patient needs to know his diagnosis. For unless he knows his life is threatened, he can scarcely be expected to fight for it.

To be denied that opportunity out of some deplorable notion of "sparing" a patient information about his own disease is tantamount to being written off as incompetent to deal with whatever life brings. The overwhelming majority of us do not want such "kindness," for it consigns us to a kind of garbage heap.

"The right to be human is non-negotiable," educator Dr. Charles Hurst said of the civil-rights movement. The right to be human also encompasses every individual's right to deny or confront his own mortality; to howl in rage over the fact that he has cancer; to be depressed by the realization that his life, like all life, must someday end; to wrestle with his bitterness over his fate; and, surprisingly often, to triumph spiritually over it by validating the unknown amount of time he has left. Cancer is a tragedy, but I have been witness to the rich variety of ways people, even the very young, can grow immeasurably because of it.

Call it respect for the individual, if you will, and believe in it, for without it your relationships have no value.

5.

Cancer
as Chronic

"Cancer is a chronic disease, not an acute,
all-or-nothing disease, and it is not always
fatal."
William N. Brand, M.D.
Director of Radiation Therapy
Northwestern Memorial Hospital
Chicago, Illinois

Dr. William Brand is examining me for the possibility of further metastases to soft tissue or bone. I stiffen against his meticulous percussion of my lungs. Thump-thump, the middle finger of his right hand taps against the middle finger of his left hand, just above the knuckle. It is the classic diagnostic technique which, when conducted by a skilled physician, can detect changes in density in deeply situated organs, such as lungs, liver, spleen, or bladder.

Satisfied with this part of his examination, Dr. Brand curves the fingers of his right hand into a soft fist and, beginning at the top of my cervical spine, pounds lightly down over each vertebra, searching for bone tenderness. It is an equally methodical procedure with frequent repetitions over bone just examined, and it fills me with apprehension: what new signs of invasive tumor will he find today? I tense against anxiety and am instantly urged to relax. Impossible when I'm tuned to signals from his hands (a repeated return to a particular inch of bone) that will produce further evidence of suspicious areas. I relax in the only way

I know: I become objective and ask a journalist's question.

"Bill, what do you think will break the stigma of cancer?"

"If everyone had it," he says without losing a beat. "If it were universal. Or, if everybody could accept the fact that they are all going to die someday. Because cancer is perhaps more curable than heart disease, more curable than a bad liver, more curable than multiple sclerosis. But it is associated so much with instant death. People think, 'I've got cancer. I'm dead.'

"Can you imagine what happens when a patient is told, 'We've found a nodule in your prostate'? Instant panic. The reality is that this man is healthy; he is functioning. His fantasy is, 'My life is over.' Certainly men have an awesome fear of coronaries, especially men who have had one and know they can easily have another. But cancer inspires more unrealistic fears and fantasies than any other disease.

"Cancer is a chronic disease, not an acute, all-or-nothing disease, and it is not always fatal. If that could be understood and accepted, then I think a lot of the prejudice against people who have had cancer would diminish. But all our lives we hear from friends, 'If I ever got cancer I would want to die right away. That's *it*.' Yet I have never seen anyone who really wanted to die.

"People cling to life. They don't give up. Remember Churchill's comment about life? Something like: It's rotten but consider the alternative. People may fake giving up to draw attention from their families or friends, something they can't get from other sources. But I don't think they ever *want* to give up until it becomes obvious to them that they can't hold on any more. When they reach that awareness—that life is ending—it's different. But for most of our patients the end is a long way off. So one doesn't see them give up. That's just contrary to the human being inside us all."

That was my introduction to the concept and reality of chronic cancer. At first, I thought it was just one man's personal position. But in the months that followed, while I was crisscrossing the country interviewing cancer specialists, gaining knowledge to write this book, I learned about the chronic nature of cancer from every medical and radiation oncologist I interviewed.

I have never heard oncologists use the word *cure* except in relation to five-year survival rates.[1] Oncologists, with their specialized knowledge of cancer, recognize that anyone who has had one experience with the disease is a candidate for recurrence, even though years may pass with no visible signs of cancer and a normal life span may be achieved. Hubert Humphrey was a classic example of an individual who had chronic cancer with remarkably long time spans between its initial diagnosis and treatment and its recurrence.

Nothing is more natural than a doctor's wish to give his patients hope. But statements such as, "We got it all," or, "If you do not have a recurrence of cancer in the next five years, consider yourself cured," can be disastrous, because they promise something which cannot be promised. Patients who have lost a sexual part of themselves, say a breast to radical mastectomy, are particularly vulnerable, for if the immense personal loss does not yield an irrevocable "cure," then what was the point of their sacrifice?

"Think of the intense disappointment and depression patients promised 'cure' feel if they have a recurrence of cancer in the sixth or the tenth or whatever year," Bill Brand said to me. "For the first five years they live on edge daily, fearing recurrence before the so-called magic five-year mark. They reach that and they celebrate. But then if cancer again reveals itself, the promise of cure is not merely a broken promise but an incredibly cruel blow. The truth is that cancer is a chronic disease; it *can* recur. And people can have two cancers.[2] But from your own experience, Jory, you know that people can learn to tolerate the disease as chronic and even feel more hopeful because of the good implications of chronicity."

The current medical trend of using the word "cure" without revealing that by "cure" a doctor means five years of disease-free survival, is not only unfair but likely to boomerang and destroy our confidence in the honesty of doctors. We patients hear "cure" and believe it means that if we live five years without recurrence, we will live the rest of our lives free of cancer. The discrepancy in meaning is just tragic; what we assume to be true may in our case be false. Though many of us who are treated for cancer never experience a recurrence, no doctor can guarantee any individual patient the hoped-for total cure. That is the fallacy of "cure," a statistical reality that defies individuation.

Dr. Vincent DeVita, Jr. director of the National Cancer Institute, in Bethesda, Maryland, and I have discussed "cure" more than once. "You have to acknowledge our interpretation of the word 'cure,'" I insist.

"I have to convince physicians that the disease is not hopeless," he replies. "That many patients now survive five years or more is a genuine advance. Optimism is possible, and patients deserve optimistic doctors."

But, as I said to Dr. DeVita, there is also genuine optimism in understanding the chronic nature of cancer. We do not begin to die immediately on being treated for the disease. We make a comeback. If the disease recurs, we build on our knowledge of the first comeback and make a second one. And a third, and a fourth, whatever it takes. The whole point is that one doesn't give up at the outset. The reason I want cancer patients to be treated by oncologists is because cancer specialists know that even if one kind of treatment fails, another may not. Their medical knowledge helps us attain a more sensible, less hysterical reaction to the word *cancer* and proves to us that when cancer is detected early enough it is simply not an all-or-nothing disease. It is a chronic disease that can be treated and held in check for years. Even for patients with very advanced stages of the disease, oncologists can virtually always "do something."

My father was a gynecologist-obstetrician of the old school. He began his medical training before World War I and took his specialized training in the 1920s, when cancer was a nearly hopeless disease, with perhaps only one patient in ten living five years after the initial diagnosis. He performed mastectomies and hysterectomies but never openly discussed cancer at home.

My father and mother referred to cancer by whispering its

medical abbreviation, CA, which is pronounced as two separate letters: "c a." The gravity of CA was such that when my father told my mother of a patient or friend who had CA, his voice was hushed. In fact, it was a secret that my grandfather, who lived with us, was himself dying of cancer. It was years before we grandchildren learned the truth. Fear, shame, and guilt over medical helplessness created walls of silence which neither our grandfather nor the rest of the family could penetrate. What everyone failed to recognize, apparently, was that my grandfather had lived with chronic cancer for years. Part of his stomach had been removed because of cancer when he was a much younger man, yet he continued to live a vigorous life until his last year, and when he died he was close to seventy.

The nature of cancer has not changed, but the ways it can be treated have. Radiation as treatment began in about 1905, but it was primitive and in many ways destructive. Modern radiation therapy equipment, precision equipment that can unerringly beam an exact dose of radiation into an exact area, was not developed until after World War II.

The first practical chemotherapy for the hematologic (blood) cancers was wrestled into existence in 1948. In the early 1950s it was applied to solid tumors—clusters of trillions of cells that form a tumor mass.

The first patients to receive chemotherapy paid a price on our behalf: they gained a few more weeks or a few more months of life in return for harsh treatment that offered no promises and may often have been more intolerable than the disease itself. But by patients' willingness to try *anything* that offered some hope, and parents' insistence that whatever was available be tried on their children, considerable progress in the treatment of some cancers has been made.[3]

The impact of a diagnosis of cancer is horrific because we are so convinced the diagnosis means we are about to die. If we could only grasp the reality of chronic cancer, we could reduce our hysteria and fear.

Our national emphasis on early detection is vital, not because early detection leads to absolute cures—no one, including the

American Cancer Society, can even begin to guarantee that—but because it offers the best chance of effective treatment.

Early detection is essential, but so are early evaluation and diagnostic work-up before surgery (staging), and the attention of an oncologist before surgery (if surgery is indicated). For no surgeon can guarantee the statement, "We got it all"; he can only guarantee he got all he could see. If everyone who receives a diagnosis of cancer would seek a second opinion from a medical oncologist immediately, then, as the ACS says, lives would be saved (or at least greatly prolonged). The real hope for all of us diagnosed as having cancer is the chance to live with the disease as a chronic illness that can be controlled by cancer specialists.

The concept and reality of chronic cancer are the essence of hope: a lucid awareness of living with cancer, living despite cancer, not dying of cancer yet. To get back on our feet after our first confrontation with the disease is a monumental victory. If, later, we have a recurrence, we will be stunned and bitter for a time, but the fact of the initial victory is a triumph and will encourage us: *I beat cancer once, I can do it again.* That is the optimism inherent in understanding cancer as a chronic disease. The only other view (cancer as an always acute disease) gives us just one chance to survive the diagnosis. Gradually, we learn something the public and those doctors who predict life span do not understand: that though we may ultimately die because of the disease, the end is not inevitably in sight at the beginning.

I abhor the implicit arrogance of, "I give you six months."[4] If a doctor can give six months, then why not be more generous and give six years? Is it really fair to risk our time span creating the possibility of a self-fulfilling prophecy? Though some patients badger doctors for specific time limits and will even keep changing doctors until they find one who will predict the unpredictable, it seems to me that the medical profession could take a united stand and insist that cancer is an open-ended disease. That is medical reality.

Oncologists have seen too many individuals with advanced cancer respond to chemotherapy and become not merely free of the aura of death but able to find life worthwhile again. The great initial enthusiasm for Interferon came precisely because Interferon achieved reversals for some patients with certain kinds of cancers.

Medical oncologists now have dozens of different drugs with which to alter the course of cancer; radiation oncologists have advanced from simple x-ray machines to powerful linear accelerators and, more recently, "particle beams" (neutron therapy). The goal is to extend life that a patient considers worthwhile, not give up because a tumor is inoperable or accept the finality of death at the start.

I knew almost nothing about cancer or oncology the first year after my diagnosis and surgery. Even after the first terrible bout with metastases was treated by oncologists, I went back to one of my old physicians. What I went to him for was mismanaged, and in desperation I returned to the medical oncologist who had treated me, and I put myself entirely in his hands. Now I have lived almost seven years with chronic and irreversible cancer. I have been extremely ill several times. I have felt I was dying several times. I have made a comeback each time. My life is not depressing; it is invigorating.

Living with chronic cancer means occasional retreats from the mainstream, during periods of intense pain and treatment, but it does not mean permanent separation from the human race. People who have chronic cancer continue to raise their children, work, eat in restaurants, go to the movies, love and make love, and travel. The experience of cancer has, of course, changed us. We have had to come to grips with our mortality, and are stronger for that. We have had to determine our priorities and focus our energies accordingly. But, having stared death in the face, we have an infinitely deeper understanding of life.

So we say to ourselves, *I'm not dead yet. I'm not dying now. This isn't what I wanted my life to be, but I've got my life. I've known unholy fear, I'm exhausted by the disease, I'm frustrated by the limitations it forces on me, but I'm still here, alive, and I've got some kind of time.*

6.

Alternatives, Choices, and Informed Consent

"The patient is the master of his or her own person. . . ."
The Doctrine of Informed Consent

"The surgeon told us that if we wanted a second opinion, we needn't come back."

"The doctor told my husband that surgery was his only hope, that radiation therapy is for fools."

"I wish your columns had appeared three weeks earlier. My wife and I did not know about possible options to mastectomy and were never informed."

Most of us never know we might have choices. Told we have cancer and devastated by the news, we numbly accept a surgeon's "I'm scheduling you for surgery the day after tomorrow" without question. For we associate surgery,[1] no matter how revolting its consequences, with the first medical "attack" on cancer. Most people—even doctors, who ought to know better—believe that radical surgery is the only definitive treatment for cancer, and that other forms of treatment are only adjuncts.[2]

Until fairly recently, this was true. A surgeon's careful

excision of the malignancy that he could see, along with extensive removal of surrounding normal tissue (including adjacent lymph nodes), was the patient's only hope. Medical knowledge of occult metastases[3] and the ability to detect them stem from quite recent discoveries. Chemotherapy, radiation therapy, hormonal therapy, immunotherapy (this last still in its infancy) are all relatively new, so it is not surprising that most doctors and the public regard them solely as therapies to follow surgery. Yet for many kinds of cancer a nonsurgical form of treatment may be a better primary treatment; for many women with breast cancer, radiation therapy as the primary treatment will obviate the need for mastectomy.[4]

As you would expect, the group of physicians likely to be the most flexible *as a group* about treatment options are the oncologists. The group likely to be least open-minded *as a group* are surgeons. Though clearly these specialists know less than oncologists about cancer and its treatment, they are, by and large, so opinionated about surgery as "the treatment of choice" that they do not really consider alternatives or choices. To them, radical surgery is a universal necessity.[5] What with their prosurgery bias and pressures to keep abreast of changes in their own specialty, they rarely read the medical literature of other specialties—and when they do, they may not believe what they read, or appreciate its importance.[6]

I have attended enough tumor board conferences, grand rounds, and postgraduate seminars on contemporary treatment of neoplasms (malignancies), and have interviewed enough physicians, to know that most doctors simply do not trust the accumulating clinical evidence for radiation therapy as primary treatment for many of the cancers located outside the abdominal cavity. I have watched doctors listen with little enthusiasm to the careful presentations made by distinguished heads of radiation oncology departments and leave the conferences and lectures unconvinced, and uninterested in learning more. Their medical prejudices are fixed: radiation is a last resort—when surgery has failed and metastases are known to exist.

We who have cancer pay a terrible price for this medical reluctance to accept change. Legally, in our society, only children and mental incompetents are refused permission to share in decisions that will affect the rest of their lives. Thus, where a choice exists but we are not told about it, or expected to discuss or participate in making the choice, we are duped. Later, when we learn how we were euchred, our faith in our doctor (and our family) turns into anger and despair.

We all know cancer patients, healed or struggling with metastatic cancer, who are so chronically depressed that we cannot bear to be with them. Until now their depression has been attributed to the paralyzing terror of cancer itself, or to depression that affected their personalities years before cancer ever occurred. But my readers furnish ample testimony to the crushing effects of doctors' cool medical detachment from patients. For every superb physician who has no trouble making contact with his patients, there is, apparently, a counterpart who can treat only the disease, not the person who has the disease.

I think of my own surgeon who told me that other women "accommodated very well to breast loss," as if my feelings about the loss of my breasts were somehow different from those of other women.[7] Reality was otherwise. Women simply are great actresses in front of their physicians.

I think of author Cornelius Ryan's description of the day he sat with his wife in a urologist's office, hearing the diagnosis of his prostate cancer, and then being told coldly that after surgery, "You will be impotent, and there is about a 20 percent chance that you will have some incontinence, varying from slight to total. If it occurs, you will require a rubber bag device which would be strapped on to catch the urine."[8]

Mr. Ryan, with an intelligent journalist's interest in getting all the facts, tried to learn about alternatives. The doctor was offended by his questions, "a sudden anger . . . surfaced quickly. . . . He launched into a curious monologue in which he referred to other urologists as 'my opponents' . . . [who] would tell us to opt for . . . radiation therapy, a treatment he contemptuously dismissed. . . . 'There is no alternative,' he said flatly," and then tried to press Ryan into having surgery two days later. When husband and wife tried to learn if time were that much of the essence, the doctor said, "You are illogical. . . . You're an educated man. I'm sure you can adjust to the trauma of the sex part of this. After all, you and your wife are surely not expecting any more children."[9]

A reader of my column in a distant city, whose brother was being pressured into immediate surgery for cancer of the larynx, remembered I once wrote that laryngectomy is often unnecessary; present-day radiation therapy can eliminate cancer as effectively as surgery in many cases, while preserving the voice box and vocal cords. Frantically, this man phoned a friend in Chicago and asked him to locate me. The Chicagoan kept making phone calls until he found someone at a television station who knew me and could be persuaded to give him my unlisted phone number. The reader's question: Could I refer his brother to a radiation oncologist? I could, and I did, but during the two days needed to locate me the surgeon threw the fear of God into the brother with cancer, so all the effort to learn about alternatives was in vain. The brother had already signed a consent to surgery, a consent that was uninformed and was obtained under duress.

These examples are not unique; I hear of similar experiences every week. Nor do I believe that the present bias in favor of radical surgery as the primary treatment is likely to shift until we who have cancer muster the courage to insist on our medical right to second opinions from cancer specialists, particularly from medical oncologists or radiation therapists (also called radiation oncologists).

Too few of us know or are informed that, though not for cancers in abdominal-cavity organs (for which surgery still is the treatment of choice), competent radiation therapy can now offer equally if not more effective primary treatment for cancers of the lip, tongue, mouth, larynx, vocal cords, breast, and genitourinary tract (in the prostate, for example), and for gynecological cancers (including labial and clitoral cancers). On a more experimental basis, primary radiation therapy is also proving its worth as an alternative to amputation for soft-tissue sarcomas of the extremities. The now-massive medical literature of radiation therapy offers ample proof of its success: for example, for cancer of the cervix there is no difference. When radiation therapy is the primary treatment, there will be almost no recurrence of cancer at the original site, and, furthermore, patients will still have intact or nearly intact physical function, and obviously intact, unmutilated bodies. Radiation treatment is generally well tolerated, and the complication rate is low.

I once compiled a five-page bibliography of current medical literature on surgery and radiation therapy in the treatment of breast cancer. The bibliography was for women who are told that mastectomy is "the only way to go—radiation therapy will shrivel your breasts." I feel that women have every right to know the facts and to have access to medical photographs showing that breasts cleared of cancer with radiation can look the same as they did before treatment, except for the small surgical scar left from removal of the tumor itself. I still receive letters from women threatened by mastectomy and from their husbands asking for the bibliography.[10] Though most of the material is technical and hard going, the photographs, survival curves, and low-rate-of-recurrence-at-original-site charts can usually be read without a medical librarian's help.

Part of the terror of cancer comes from our awareness that we will probably be rushed into surgery the minute the diagnosis is confirmed. One way to lessen this particular fear is to accept the real truth of the matter: that by the time we have recognizable symptoms, our cancer may be several years old. Nobody knows how or when cancer begins, only that the controls that keep cells dividing normally are lost, leaving cells to themselves to replicate in crazy, haphazard patterns. One cell grows into an abnormality and divides, becoming two kinky cells; two become four; four eight; on and on to trillions of aberrant cells which become a large mass of cells (a tumor). Eventually, the mass will become large enough to be detected, but it may take years.

The cells will continue to multiply; the cancer will attempt to spread and, indeed, may do so before the primary tumor is recognized. But the new pea-sized lump a man or woman suddenly feels will not become the size of a golf ball overnight. A patient in the hands of a cancer specialist has enough time for a whole range of diagnostic procedures to be made in order to *stage* the cancer, that is, to determine how far it has progressed. This work-up (testing) period gives a patient enough time to explore alternatives, to get a second opinion and a third opinion, and a fourth and fifth, if that seems necessary.

The major exceptions are those few cancers that are excessively virulent and the cancers that can clearly be diagnosed and described as long-standing undetected cancers. Failure to detect cancer is often the fault of the individual who suspected cancer but was afraid to learn the truth, and kept postponing medical examination.[11] Thus, he closed off his options, for one of the great benefits of early diagnosis is detection at a stage when alternatives less mutilative than surgery are often equally effective.

In this country and elsewhere, the tendency is to refer newly diagnosed cancer patients immediately to surgeons. Only much later, if cancer recurs, are these "failed" patients referred to cancer specialists. That is just crazy. With a disease as complicated and baffling as cancer, it is in our own best interests to insist that a cancer specialist be our specialist from the start.

Beginning in mid-May, 1978, I wrote four successive columns on "Breast Removal and Uninformed Consent."[12] In late July, I received a letter from Irving Rimer, Vice President for Public Information of the American Cancer Society: "I know that many physicians will be exercised [sic] over your comments on treatments for breast cancer. Knowing that the great majority of women will experience surgery, it is important to give them confidence in the procedures. Most people don't have the choices you cite. . . ."

The letter presents a very odd point of view. In the first place, the problem isn't lack of confidence in the procedure but lack of confidence in the decision for surgery. In the second place, almost everyone has access to either a hospital with a cancer center or a state university medical center with a department of radiation therapy. Women who wish to learn if their breasts can be saved are perfectly capable of making the necessary trip; many now cross the country to get second opinions from radiation-therapy department heads whose names and reputations they already know. In any event, I felt my readers would be buoyed by the kinds of letters I was receiving from oncologists who had read the May columns, so in August I wrote two wrap-up columns containing excerpts from those letters.[13]

Now as then, what bothers me most is resistance to change when change can mean a less traumatic cancer experience. Doctors who insist that surgery is the only possible treatment for breast cancer err. The various types of breast cancers are among the meanest cancers, and, despite the different surgical procedures for them, the statistics on women who survive breast cancer have scarcely changed in the last forty-five years. Hence, "I've been doing this procedure for ten years (or twenty years, or whatever), and it's the best way to go," means only that it is best from the surgeon's viewpoint. Most women never fully recover from the psychological damage of mastectomy, and, if they are subjected to the now-outmoded Halsted radicals[14] or the supra-radicals,[15] they must be magnificent actresses if they can conceal from their doctors their emotional condition. If some women's breasts can be saved, the least a doctor can do is help his patient learn whether in her case it is possible. That decision should be shared with a radiation oncologist, a medical colleague. If the radiation oncologist says to a woman, "I'm sorry, but because of the position of your tumor, a mastectomy will be necessary," that woman will find it easier to accept the mastectomy and will have far more trust in the doctor who looked for an alternative. And her signature on the surgical consent form more likely will be an honest, unforced consent.

As a doctrine and as a practical reality, informed consent is neither so complicated nor so difficult as doctors and lawyers would make it, nor is there any good reason for the extended medical debates it engenders. At its core, it is respect for a patient as an individual, not a defense against the possibility of a later malpractice suit.

The doctrine of informed consent is an ethical issue. A doctor who has taken the Hippocratic oath, accepting its admonition to "do no harm," has an obligation to recognize that he harms a cancer patient if he neglects to inform that patient of alternatives, or if he presents the alternatives with so much bias that the patient is covertly coerced out of his options. A doctor whose own ox is not being gored too often dismisses this point as of little consequence. My own feeling is that when we meet such a doctor, we should immediately leave him.

Informed consent is not just our signature on a hospital consent form stating our willingness to permit "diagnosis and medical treatment . . . diagnostic procedures, x-ray, nuclear, electrical, and laboratory tests or treatment, or blood transfusion." It is not a piece of paper casually obtained from us by our physician's resident or a nurse the night before our surgery or the start of other treatment. Informed consent means that our physician has spent time discussing with us "1) the procedure, 2) its purpose, 3) risks, 4) likely consequences with and without treatment, 5) alternatives available, 6) advantages and disadvantages of one course of treatment over another."[16] To these we might well add: 7) the physician's recommendation and reasons why.

The doctrine of informed consent recognizes each patient as an individual who, though probably medically unsophisticated and most certainly vulnerable because of fear, is still capable of absorbing information and coming to a decision that is in his best interest.[17] Though many patients will never challenge their physicians' recommendations, and many more will shift all decision-making responsibility to their doctors ("Anything you say, Doc"), the risk in assuming a cancer patient is unable to make decisions about his own medical treatment can be catastrophic. Witness the tremendous jump in malpractice suits of the past few years. Though plaintiffs usually sue because of irrevocable, untoward results, skimpy communication and inadequate information contribute mightily to a plaintiff's belief that he has every right to sue.

In a nation in which one out of four citizens will at some time develop cancer, in which virtually all of us know or know of someone who has cancer, and in which cancer news is "hot" mass media news, a physician's assumption that adults and adolescents newly diagnosed as having cancer are innocents about the disease is naive. The ideas new patients have about cancer may not reflect scientific acumen, but a patient's lack of precise medical knowledge should never be interpreted as lack of interest in learning about the best way of treating his disease. Nor should a patient's awkwardness or timidity in asking questions.

It is true that very few of us are easily able to face a head-on confrontation with our own mortal fragility, but, even so, most of us are not prepared to have others suddenly assume all our decision-making. That is not how we have been conducting our lives until now, and we resent the condescension of doctors, nurses, and technicians, who seem to feel we should be dealt with as rather dim kindergarteners. I think of the technician in a privately owned x-ray laboratory who said to me each time I appeared for x-rays, "Now we go in here and we take off all our clothes. . . ."

One day I stood outside the tiny dressing room and made an Alphonse-Gaston gesture with my hand. She stared at me. "After you," I said.

"Whatever are you talking about?" she asked.

"Well," I said, "if *we* take off our clothes, then this time I'll let you go first." It was one of my better moments with a disease that rarely lends itself to more than black humor.

In that same facility, on a day when I was terrified over what some chest x-rays might reveal about bone damage, I asked to see one of the two radiologists in charge. The technician asked why. "It's Friday," I said. "By the time you deliver the film to my doctor, he will have left his office for the day. I'd rather not wait until Monday to know what is wrong." The technician understood and suggested I wait in the reception room. Much later, she came out to say that the radiologist could not see me; he could only forward the films to my physician, who would surely be in touch with me. My anxiety and anger got the best of me and, in full voice, I expounded on "autocrats" who couldn't deal on a one-to-one basis with patients and who refused patients the right to learn what was wrong with their own bodies. To no avail.

On Monday afternoon, I told my physician what had happened. He said mildly, "Dr. B. didn't know you knew you had cancer."

That triggered my anger again. "Don't all your patients know they have cancer?"

He explained that many people who were referred to the x-ray facility did not know their diagnosis, that Dr. B. was a courteous old gentleman who did not wish to interfere with medical decisions made by other physicians or risk telling other doctors' patients something that might not be in their best interest. "How dare he make that decision?" I said. "It is *my* body, *my* concern over what is happening to it, *my* fear of a new onset of metastases. Doesn't that ever enter your courteous old gentleman's mind?"

Unfortunately, the refusal to deal on a one-to-one basis with a cancer patient is commonplace. The medical and paramedical attitude that says *Ask your doctor for this information* or *Your doctor will decide, your doctor will do what's best for you* is thoroughly ingrained in the entire system. Anxious patients and their equally anxious families are subjected to it continuously in ways that can only be described as inhuman.

At some point in the history of medicine, physicians came to believe they had absolute power. This probably occurred when surgery became the most talked-about and most hopeful medical specialty, raising surgeons to the top position in hospital hierarchies. The miracles the "men in white" perform—kidney transplants, coronary by-passes, reattaching severed hands to arms, intricate neurosurgical procedures—are not to be underestimated. But surgeons cannot guarantee similar miracles for cancer cases, so it would be nice to discover in them a little more humble awareness of the deep human needs of their cancer patients.

In the lead article in the *New England Journal of Medicine*, December 21, 1978, three physicians showed that when older patients with "operable" lung cancer were offered a hypothetical choice between a thoracotomy (surgery) and radiation therapy as primary treatment of their lesions, the patients overwhelmingly chose radiation therapy.[18] The reason: though radiation therapy represented a "shorter period of guaranteed certain survival . . . [surgery represented] a gamble between long-term survival and immediate death."[19] The study was as free of bias as possible and the authors' conclusions included the "importance of choosing therapies not only on the basis of objective measures of survival but also on the basis of patient attitudes."[20]

As do virtually all *New England Journal of Medicine* articles, this one prompted correspondence from the *Journal*'s audience of physicians. One published letter, from an internist at Stanford University Medical Center, suggested that "it may be worthwhile to ask the question: How good are physicians at knowing what their patients value most?"[21] Another, from a surgeon at Southern Illinois University School of Medicine began:

> In the decision-making process, the patient provides input with all the details obtained from the clinical history. Additional information comes from the results of laboratory tests and from all the knowledge obtained by the physician from his review of the medical literature and past experience. To give veto power to the patient, who has at best very little access to all this information, means that the decision is statistically less likely to be the best because of the limited data on which it is based. . . . [22]

This second viewpoint, the traditional surgeon's viewpoint, ignores one crucial fact: lung cancers are lethal, and most if not all individuals who develop lung cancer know it. Statistically, only five percent of all lung cancer patients survive five years from the time of diagnosis. Only twenty percent survive one year. The average length of survival from the time of diagnosis is a meager six to nine months.[23]

In the face of such bleak statistics, how can any doctor worthy of his M.D. make a unilateral decision to gamble with the slight time span left his lung cancer patient? The doctor cannot know if his patient will become one of the twenty percent who will live more than a year, or one of the five percent who will be productive and active five years hence. He does not have a crystal

ball. To arrogate the right to play percentages without so informing his patient is fundamentally wrong. The intent of informed
consent is precisely to give each patient veto power; and each
patient, not his doctor, must make the final decision.

Doctors simply cannot go on assuming that, because many
patients want to avoid all responsibility for life and death decisions ("You decide, Doc"), no patients wish to direct their own
lives. Most of my column readers believe that the assumption of
risk and the right to choose and decide are matters of *their*
autonomy, *their* responsibility.

"The patient is the master of his or her own person." Informed
consent is not just a theory, nor is it a token gesture, a toy to be
withheld by those who would play God. It is each patient's
absolute right, assigned by ethics, justice, the law, and our
humanitarian traditions. With his expectations, with his pain, with
his life, and with his money, the patient is the one who will pay.
To him who pays belongs the right to call the tune.

7.

Trust

"If I tell you, you trust me. . . ."
John M. Merrill, M.D.
Associate Professor of Clinical Medicine
Northwestern University Medical School

An anonymous reader once sent me a sheet of paper on which he had printed in big, purple letters, YOU FEAR DOCTORS, thereby giving me my chuckle for the day. He also gave me something to think about, for his ink was the exact shade of purple used in the Roman Catholic church. I began musing about "Papa," the Italian word for the pope, and "Father" for priests, and how physicians, too, become father figures when we are under stress.

If, in our earliest childhood, we had the advantage of good fathers, we learned about being protected. We were loved, cared for, and wrapped in paternalism when we needed it most by a father we could trust to be there for us when we were hurt. That father would take us in his arms, deal with our hurt, and promise to make it go away.

Now, in our time of biggest hurt and deepest need, we unconsciously transfer to our doctor our primal need for the godlike father of our childhood. Neither we nor our doctor is aware of the degree to which that early childhood faith engulfs us and is projected onto him. Nor can either of us prevent this from occurring; it happens simply because our need is so great.

When cancer is suspected, we usually become patients of doctors whom we have never seen. The first of these strangers generally is a surgeon to whom we are referred for a diagnosis. Tense with anxiety, we bring to our initial meeting with him the unrecognized expectation that he will behave as we recall our godlike father did. We do not ask this doctor if he wants that role. We confer it on him and assume he will accept the responsibility of our trust and need.

Our trust can be his greatest asset, for he can use it to create hope. He also can abuse it, in either an active or a passive way. The first urologist that author Cornelius Ryan saw is a classic example of a man actively abusing trust. Mr. Ryan came to him hoping for hope; the urologist coldly sliced through every level of confidence. I shall always admire Mr. Ryan for refusing to be defeated by that overwhelming breach of faith. Many people are simply too intimidated by their disease or their doctor to say, "Sorry, but you are not the right doctor for me."

The surgeon who first treated me breached trust passively, by withholding facts. I did not know for more than two years after his initial diagnosis of breast cancer that, at the time of my surgery, he had found more than one involved lymph node and that my life was very much in peril. This surgeon, a kindly man but an old-school pessimist who viewed metastatic cancer as swift doom, believed that since I was already traumatized by breast loss, he should withhold certain details. When I finally learned that details had been withheld, my faith in him collapsed.

Shattered trust wounds cruelly under any circumstances, but never more so than when we have cancer. At other times in our lives, we learned we could survive broken love, job loss, or the suddenly corrupt behavior of a friend in whom we had every confidence. We struggled through the pain of divorce, the ache of a parent's death, the humiliation of a personal bankruptcy, the deep hurt when a nearly adult child stormed out of our lives.

Cancer is not like any of these defeats. Cancer shoves us to a precipice: on this side, life; below us, death. Alone, we cannot back away from the brink. *I need a hand to hold.*

The hand we most want to hold belongs to our physician, for only he can offer what Dr. Avery Danto Weisman, a prominent Harvard Medical School psychiatrist and a giant of compassion and understanding, calls "safe conduct." He defines safe conduct as "that dimension beyond diagnosis, treatment, and relief which refers to how a physician will conduct a patient through a maze of uncertain, perplexing, and distressing events. . . ."[1]

A doctor who understands the individual catastrophe of cancer, and who acts accordingly, does indeed take our hand and offer safe conduct. This is the essence of the physician-patient relationship, and it is based solely on trust.

Trust was the essence of our childhood bond to our parents, but trust is fragile and comes into question as we mature. Part of growing up, after all, is learning to relinquish blind trust in our parents. If, because of fear and need, we unconsciously transfer the blind trust of childhood onto physicians, we are bound to be disappointed in them.

We need to distinguish blind trust from realistic faith in doctors, and I have discovered that with cancer we need to question ourselves and evaluate our expectations of doctors time and again. Otherwise, we may expect our doctors to meet the emotional demands we made of our fathers, and that is not something they can do.

On the other hand, we have every right to expect our doctors to provide solid information about our kind of cancer and all its identifiable locations, full disclosure of both the diagnostic and therapeutic treatment plans they have in mind, and safe conduct throughout our illness and treatment.[2] Failure to disclose fully— for example, failure to reveal anything but the first step in a planned sequence of procedures—amounts to leading us up the garden path, and that is wrong. For later, when we are informed that another unpleasant step must now be taken, that the first step was only the beginning, we justifiably feel betrayed.

But when our physician is open, when he says, "We're going to begin with this approach, which includes the following . . . and if we need to do more, we'll do the following," our confidence in him almost never lags. His program outline may chill us because, as he admits, it is aggressive treatment, but by meeting us as equals, he unites us with him in the fight against the disease. And in revealing his back-up plans, he demonstrates that we are not locked into a single, win-or-lose method of treatment. From such awareness, courage to fight the disease is born. And so is hope.

Oncologists are more likely to be open in dealing with cancer than other specialists because of their greater knowledge of treatment possibilities, but that is no guarantee that they will be. My dismay with close-mouthed oncologists is the same as with physicians in other specialties; if they repeatedly break faith, we have every right to look for a cancer specialist we can trust. The threats and defeats of cancer, especially advancing cancer, are too formidable for us to cope with alone. A supportive and understanding family can make an enormous difference, but we also desperately need our doctor to understand what we are going through.

Adult trust builds slowly. We come to trust our physician when we have confidence in his medical competence and judgement, faith in his honesty and openness, and the conviction that he does not withhold information. Trust means we *know* that if he has a personal or medical bias for one form of treatment over another, he will tell us so. From our prior experiences with him, we are also certain that whatever he tells us will be told in a considerate way.

If we have advanced cancer, we need to know we will have safe conduct to the very end. Throughout the dangerous journey, there will be times when we disagree with our doctor, oppose him, and even (unfairly) lash out at him as if he were responsible for giving us our disease.[3] A wise doctor understands that kind of anger and frustration and realizes that lashing-out and blaming will pass. He continues to uphold our right to ask questions, hear answers, and refuse treatment, though we may be narrowing our future options or our life span.

I may have shortened my life span by refusing chemotherapy for almost six years. My oncologist, Dr. John Merrill, did not like my decision; he felt it was medically wrong. But he understood my need to work with as clear a head and as little chemical-caused exhaustion as possible, and so he proposed an alternative treatment which could also buy me some time: hormonal ablation therapy[4] through removal of ovarian function. Again we differed. Dr. Merrill wanted surgical removal of my ovaries; I asked for their destruction through irradiation, and explained why.[5] He agreed, albeit reluctantly, but in so doing won my confidence and respect. Clearly, he had accepted me as an individual and acknowledged that my needs could take precedence over his best medical judgement. He was willing to be flexible, and he remained calm. That is how we became partners in controlling my disease.

My relationship with John Merrill is one kind of trusting relationship—mutual trust. The other kind is dependent trust. In a situation of dependent trust, a patient says, in effect, "My doctor understands me. He knows my symptoms. He tells me the truth. He will help me, but I don't have to get involved in decision-making because I trust him to make the right decision for me."

Mutual trust and dependent trust are each good in their own ways. But mutual trust, with its sense of *we are a team,* is better. When there is mutual trust our wishes will be heard. We will be neither passive nor helpless, but full participants in all medical decisions that affect us. (Realistically, because of our right to refuse treatment, we have the decisive vote.) Though we will be frustrated by our disease, we will not be frustrated by our doctors, and we will never be in the position of the patients who write to me saying:

"I resent the doctors ignoring my questions or directing their answers to others like I am an idiot or a child. . . ."

"If I ask too many questions, I am accused of being 'too upset' or 'too emotional to handle my problem.' But it is my *problem, it's cancer in* me. . . ."

"I bring my physicians a list of questions, and I'm told I am in good hands, they are doing their best, and I'm not supposed to delve so

deeply into the nature of my cancer because it will prey on my mind. Who are they kidding? I have cancer and it is on my mind. . . ."

These are not three isolated and unfortunate experiences. Rather, they stand for a kind of despair I hear almost every day.

We do not want such doctors. We want oncologists like the one who said, "Give me a patient who is fighting mad [over having cancer] and, together, that patient and I have a chance." We need oncologists like John Merrill, who once shyly admitted to me that he had put himself through a thoroughly painful bone-marrow test to learn what his patients have to endure when he orders a bone-marrow test for them. We need oncologists who can inspire in us the kind of confidence that led one patient to say to his radiation oncologist, "I think I'm going to get well." When the oncologist asked why, the patient said, "Because of the way you do things."

Physicians talk about "management of the cancer patient," but to many of them "management" means medical control of the disease and excludes ideas of, say, *listening* to a patient's confession of loss of courage and then buoying his patient's feelings. The failure to provide safe conduct is the most serious shortcoming in cancer treatment today.[6]

Some patients are brave enough to challenge a doctor who lets them down, but most feel inadequate to speak up on their own behalf. For if their doctor rejects them, where will they turn for the crucial help needed to maintain their life? More than most other patients, cancer patients are disadvantaged in their relationships with their doctors because of the corrosive emotional stresses that accompany their disease. And so, for too many of them, the tiniest occasional gesture of personal concern from their physician invokes teary gratitude. How I wish these patients could realize that they have the right to ask for and receive more than minimal emotional support.

The inadequate physician is not often recognized or described as such. Instead, his patients repeatedly make incredible allowances for his poor performance. For example: "I know he is busy and has only a minute to see me."

Whenever I hear this pathetic defense of a doctor who is failing his patient and breaching his patient's trust, I think of the man who wrote to me:

> When my wife was referred by her eye doctor, it was to an internist who runs a medical factory and sees close to a hundred patients a day. His wife, who works in his office, tells patients they must pay immediately (she collects the money) and that they must fill out all their own insurance papers. My wife has seen this doctor several times, and each time he sent her home saying the dizziness and headaches and all other problems were psychosomatic. Later, after neurosurgery, it was revealed [that] a brain tumor [was the cause]. . . .

Who, in any similar but nonmedical situation, would put up with such unconscionable behavior?

When we are angry at or distrustful of authority figures in other fields, we speak up. If we think we are right and they are wrong, we argue with policemen, protest to judges, confront school principals on behalf of our children, and write angry letters to our congressmen, to presidents of corporations, and to the president of our country.

When a lawyer or an income tax expert or a banker lets us down, we are not afraid to say so. We know there are other lawyers and tax experts and bankers to help us, even if we have to travel from a small town to a city to find them. Similarly, most of us can travel beyond a small town's city limits to find a cancer specialist who inspires confidence. It's just tragic so few of us do.

In his memoirs, Sir Sidney Smith, one of the great forensic pathologists of our time, tells of earning a scholarship to the University of Edinburgh and sailing from his boyhood home in New Zealand halfway around the world to Scotland. During medical school he worked at a medical post in Fife. One of his first patients was a young woman who was pregnant, suffering from continuous convulsions, and dying. Young Sidney Smith desperately tried every available drug to stop her convulsions, but all were futile. "She died holding my hand, thanking me for all I had done."[7] The experience changed his life. When he returned to the University of Edinburgh, he knew he could not graduate as a clinician, for the direct involvement with patients which is clinical medicine means enduring feelings of helplessness when one's patients die. With the dean's help, he shifted his focus, graduating with honors (1912) as a brilliant young pathologist.

Alas, not many doctors discover early enough in their medical careers that they are beyond their emotional depths. If they cannot tolerate the degree of trust implicit in physician-patient relationships, they ought to get out of clinical medicine and into research, where they will not have to deal with patients. Instead, too many harden their hearts and allow submissive patients to pay the price.

The following letter from a reader sums up safe conduct and trust so well. In this instance a patient's wife refused to accept the bleak finality of doctors who were emotionally bankrupt:

Dear Jory:
I want to thank you for your column of July 15 [1979], "No Conflict Between God and Physicians." I called the telephone number you listed[8] and found that a cancer specialist is [called] an oncologist.

My husband, 54, was operated on for cancer of the pancreas on May 30 of this year. He had no symptoms until May 13. We had been leading a full, active life until then.

The doctors gave no hope. Recommended no therapy—it would only make him sicker—average time of survival is six months. I was told to just be cheerful and keep up his spirits and keep all this information from him. Don't they know [that] after living together for 29 years, [it] is impossible to start keeping secrets from one another?

I told my husband in the gentlest way I could that there would be no treatment, and that six months was all the time he had. We cried together, and he accepted it. He's a friendly, outgoing, optimistic person. Learning he had cancer came as a shock to him, but he said he would beat it.

After finding an oncologist: more tests; transfer of medical records and slides; another pathologist thinks that instead of pancreatic cancer it may be lymph node cancer [lymphoma], which is more responsive to treatment.

We are full of hope that this may be the case. Even if it proves to be pancreatic cancer, the oncologist believes that since my husband is ambulatory he should get chemotherapy, that he may be in the 15 percent that do respond.

He may start treatment tomorrow if new test results are in.

I don't know why the surgeon and other doctors did not refer us to a cancer specialist, except that they told me that it was too large a tumor and too involved in other vital organs.

Your column has given us new hope and we want to thank you for this. . . .

No patient, no family facing cancer, should ever hear, "There is no hope." That is just devastating. So is the number of lives dismissed out of hand by doctors who destroy hope because their egos will not allow them to consult with cancer specialists.

The capacity for compassion is within everyone's scope, and every human being can discover it within himself.[9] Basically, it begins with sensitivity to others, *their* wishes, *their* problems, *their* needs.

So often the need is for a different way of perceiving our situation. For example: After almost six years of living with cancer, I finally had to accept chemotherapy as the only way to keep from dying prematurely. For the first months, the chemicals made me incredibly ill. One day after John Merrill had examined me, I wailed that I couldn't bear his treatment any longer, that it was destroying me for fourteen of every twenty-eight days. "I'm too ill to enjoy anything, too ill to work, too wiped out to lead any normal social life. I'm not sure this half-living is worth anything. I'm not sure I want the little that's left." John began to say, "Many of my patients develop tolerance for their treatment. You may, you know." But his statement seemed inconsequential, I was that immersed in self-pity and tears. He left, and a nurse I had not seen before came in to give me my injection. Taking one look at me, she kindly asked what was wrong. I repeated, "I might as well let go now and die, I'm certainly not living fourteen days out of every twenty-eight."

"Or, you might say you're gaining fourteen days every four weeks." She stopped my tears with that one.

I sat there thinking and scarcely felt the tiny needle she inserted into a vein in my hand. Finally, I said, "Well, you've given me a different perspective. Thank you." And all the way home I was grateful because she had just given me the gifts of caring, insight, and hope.

The ability to be *with* us emotionally as well as physically is a critical factor in cancer treatment. It is a physician's ability to care, his dedication to safe conduct, his determination to maintain his patient's trust, and his willingness to reexamine himself: *I have something to give to each of my patients. I will not be depleted by giving, though I will feel stretched thin at times. I can afford to show emotion because my strength will not be eroded through caring. I can be alert to the vulnerability of each of my patients, for if I have to harden myself against that, am I not merely denying my equal vulnerability?*

Physicians who continue to question themselves and reach this kind of inner harmony conduct their patients safely through the most terrible woes known, and their patients, even when dying, have the security of a trusting relationship to the very end. Belief in us and themselves is the unique gift physicians have to give. With that strength, we can live with cancer, not merely suffer through it.

The art of medicine requires a host of intangible qualities: acceptance, compassion, dedication, empathy, fairness, honesty, openness, and the ability to accept the demands while delighting in the rewards of trusting relationships. These qualities enable a physician to give hope, to sustain hope, and to assure safe conduct. A physician who develops his skills in the art of medicine is a healer in the best sense of the word. For a healed spirit can soar high, free of the physical limits imposed by disease and human mortality.

8.

The Right to Be Free of Pain

"No patient should ever wish for death
because of his physician's reluctance to use
adequate amounts of effective narcotics."
*Jerome Jaffe, M.D., and William Martin,
M.D.*[1]

"With care and patience, the physician can
render practically any cancer patient
pain-free."
David S. Shimm, M.D., et al.[2]

Cancer's unholy image is of prolonged suffering relieved only by
death. The dying cancer patient moans continually because of his
pain, his family begs the doctor to relieve the pain, the doctor says
regretfully, "I am sorry, I am doing all I can."

During the first two years in which I was learning to live with
cancer, this image of the ending of life shadowed my every waking
hour. I began thinking about suicide as an acceptable alternative
and made plans to end my life when pain became overwhelming.
But, by the time I began work on this book, I was no longer so
fearful or so naive. In fact, I had come to the inescapable
conclusion that the suffering of dying cancer patients which we
hear about continuously is both morally and medically inexcus-
able. I had learned that:

- as many as half of all cancer patients die in no pain or
  feeling only mild pain;
- patients who die in merciless pain are almost always
  allowed to suffer needlessly;

- freedom from excruciating pain is a reality for cancer patients who die in hospices and at cancer centers;
- nerve blocks, radiation therapy, chemotherapy, and, above all, adequate use of narcotic analgesics (morphine or methadone, for example) will free virtually every dying cancer patient from intractable pain.

The alleviation of cancer pain is no longer mysterious. The causes of pain are known. Cancer itself does not create pain. Pain comes from the obstruction by a tumor of the normal function of hollow viscera (broadly, intestines and other abdominal or thoracic organs); it comes from bone fracture or collapse as a consequence of erosion by tumor; or from the pressure of solid tumor on nerve. Lung cancer patients are in pain because they are suffocating—tumor blocks their lungs from normal oxygen supply. But the pain caused by cancer in all these sites can be reduced significantly. So it is fair to ask why so many physicians and nurses refuse to give adequate amounts of narcotics at adequate intervals and why some cancer patients and their families initially refuse their use.

The answer is threefold. The first barrier to giving adequate narcotics is voiced as fear of creating drug addiction. This fear, though thoroughly illogical in the face of approaching death, is perhaps the greatest single obstacle to effective control of a cancer patient's pain.[3]

The second barrier to the use of adequate narcotics is ignorance. The advances made in the last decade in understanding the nature of cancer pain and ways to control it are not widely known. Relatively few physicians (other than oncologists and pain specialists) have read the new literature on cancer-pain management or have attended even one continuing-medical-education seminar on pain control. Hence, most doctors are disadvantaged in effectively managing cancer pain because their drug prescribing habits are self-contradictory and obsolete.[4]

With almost any drug orders but those for narcotic drugs (narcotic analgesics) a physician specifies that a fixed amount of a drug be administered at a fixed time interval (generally three, four, or six hours) around the clock. Dependent on the drug's potency, such an order assures that a given drug's concentration in the blood will not drop to zero effectiveness before the next dose is administered. (See graph 1, illustrating drug action.) The order for this kind of drug administration is written *q4h* from the Latin *quaque quater hora,* "give every four hours." The numeral that represents the time interval in *q4h* is variable. It could be a 3, as in *q3h,* or any other time interval the doctor specifies.

But when narcotics are to be prescribed, the typical doctor tiptoes gingerly around their use and safeguards his *q4h* by adding the notation *prn. Prn,* from the Latin *pro re nata,* means "give as needed" but no more often than the interval stated in the *q—h* order. The problem with *prn* is that the determination of need is made by a nurse. Few nurses have been trained in pharmacology. Most nurses worry they will overdose. Most nurses usually assume that narcotics are more potent than they actually are. This combination of factors leads nurses to stretch the intervals of drug administration, to the point where a *q3h prn* order may be arbitrarily extended by the nurse to a *q4h* order.

If the narcotic in question can deliver only two hours of effective pain relief, a cancer patient whose pain is increasing in severity by the minute will start asking for more medication to relieve his pain soon after those two hours are up. The nurse, of course, will refuse the patient's request; according to her time-table (if she has extended a *q3h prn* order to *q4h*), two more hours must elapse before the drug can again be administered. The result is a patient suffering wholly unnecessary pain because his nurse believes his pain is under control.

Does a solution exist? It does, and it is simple. All a doctor need do is break himself of the habit of writing *prn* orders when pain relief is the prime goal. Virtually all studies of cancer-pain relief have concluded that *prn* has no place in the treatment of chronic pain, and in fact is counterproductive.

Graphs 1 and 2 show drug action for a typical patient. The horizontal scale on each graph represents the duration of drug action. As you see, pain-relieving drugs reach their peak effectiveness within the first two hours following their administration. The vertical scale on each graph represents the concentration of a drug in the bloodstream.

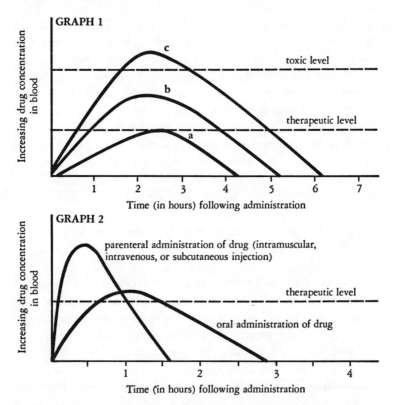

In graph 1, the letters *a, b, c* represent drugs of various potency. Drug *a* is obviously unacceptable, for it never reaches a therapeutic level. Drug *c* is toxic at its peak of action. A solution is to give drug *b*, but it must be given often enough. If given only every four or five hours, drug *b* will not control pain long enough to be effective. *Q 3h* is an appropriate order here.

Graph 2 shows the differences in onset of pain-relieving effect and completion of action between drugs administered orally and drugs administered by injection. Injected drugs reach a higher level of blood concentration but also drop rapidly from a therapeutic level. These rapid ups and downs may lead to such rapid changes in the level of pain relief that the choice of an oral drug given often enough is preferred. The goal always is to prevent the recurrence of pain. That goal is reached by administering drugs on a fixed schedule, at whatever interval gives the most constant relief.

Dr. Raymond Houde, Professor of Pharmacology at Cornell University Medical College[5] (an expert on the control of cancer pain), and I once discussed common misconceptions about narcotic use in the control of pain. He said:

"I don't think there's any reason for people to die in pain. I think that the real problem is that doctors are afraid to use medicines that are appropriate. I find that doctors have real concerns about patients' dying 'addicted,' which is absolute nonsense. It's as though doctors are afraid you're going to appear at Saint Peter's gate with alcohol on your breath."

I ventured that if one were in pain and dreaded dying, it might be helpful to be a little euphoric.

However Dr. Houde said that no one ever saw cancer patients dancing in the halls at Memorial Hospital. "In street use, drugs are a cult; dancing around is acting-out that comes along with the cult. If you saw our patients here [who are] on narcotics, you wouldn't be able to tell who was on them and who was not. Narcotics dull alertness to some extent, but, apart from that, people can function quite well. The important thing is that *people in pain can't function, either.* [Emphasis added.]

"Physicians rarely think beyond 'fixed doses,' 'usual doses,' 'average doses.' They think the 'usual dose' is the only dose. But there are no average or usual doses, because everyone has a different body size, metabolizes drugs differently, has different needs for medication. We titrate drug dosages, that is, change medication or change the amount or the way medication is given, according to each patient's needs, and that makes all the difference in successful treatment of pain."

The third barrier to adequate narcotic use is the fact that all of us—patients, families, physicians, our entire society—believe in the inevitability of cancer pain. The facts are otherwise, but most people simply do not believe them.[6] These are the facts:

According to Dr. Robert Twycross, a British clinical pharmacologist who has done much to develop many of the British hospice methods that assure pain-free dying,[7] "As many as half of all patients with terminal cancer have no pain or a negligible discomfort at most. Forty percent experience severe pain, and the remaining 10% suffer less intense pain. Furthermore, it is theoretically possible to relieve the pain in every case. Success depends on the doctor having an adequate concept of the nature of pain, an understanding of the correct use of analgesics, and links with specialist colleagues so that help can be obtained in problem cases."[8]

Dr. Kathleen M. Foley studied 36,800 patients admitted to Memorial Sloan-Kettering Cancer Center between January, 1974, and January, 1978, and produced nearly identical figures. Nine percent of the patients (4,240) "had pain of a significant magnitude and complexity to require a specific consultation from the Pain Service."[9]

Almost every one of us knows a horror story about someone whose last weeks of life were excruciating because of pain. The endless evidence of these tragic dyings has convinced us it is impossible to die of cancer pain-free. Since nobody has stepped forward in the public literature to say that excruciating pain need not be, we are convinced that it will be. Small wonder that instead of demanding that doctors do more than regret their helplessness, we meekly accept the notion that, with cancer, excruciating pain is inevitable. But the price we pay is the horrible continuation of wholly unnecessary pain.

Our American attitudes toward pain and our acceptance of pain itself are infused with irrational cultural beliefs that are centuries old. They have come down to us through our Judeo-Christian heritage, and they hold that pain is punishment for wrongdoing and sin; it is to be endured stoically; suffering is noble when borne without complaint.

From the origins of human life, pain was part of the human

condition. Primitive man knew it intimately, but his lack of scientific knowledge meant that his attempts to explain the causes of pain were pure conjecture; thus, his efforts to cure pain were almost totally hit-or-miss. For example, primitive man invented a crude form of trephining (a surgical procedure still in use, though now highly refined) because he believed that headaches, dizziness, blindness, and insanity were caused by evil spirits that somehow had gotten into the head. Primitive man let out the evil spirits by chipping or boring a hole in the head. Accidentally, he sometimes achieved a cure, at least in those instances when intracranial pressure and excess fluids were causing the headache, dizziness, blindness, or erratic behavior. Apparently, every society from the Babylonians and the earliest dynasties of China believed that a toothache was caused by a worm in the tooth. This idea lasted until the end of the eighteenth century, when some understanding of dental caries developed.

In ancient Egypt and Greece, virtually every deity was associated in some way with illness or death; each of the gods was responsible for sending or removing certain plagues, sicknesses, or pains, just as they were responsible for everything else.

The authors of the Old Testament supplied the most compelling explanation in the Western World for pain. In the third chapter of Genesis (3:16), God punishes Eve for eating the forbidden fruit. He decrees: "I will greatly multiply your pain in child-bearing; in pain you shall bring forth children."

Because Hebrew religion reformulated prior religious belief into monotheism, and had to integrate blessings and curses in a single deity, the Genesis account made creative use of earlier primal myths to explain the origin of pain. Medieval Christianity presented the cause: pain and suffering were direct consequences of the action in the Garden of Eden, the penalties for the inherently flawed nature of all humans which all of us must pay. (Thus everyone was behaviorally innocent but simultaneously condemned.)

As Reformed Christianity further elaborated on the New Testament, the theme of the worthlessness of individuals, their absolute lack of virtue, gained enormous doctrinal popularity. Now, man was viewed as utterly wretched, doomed to suffer not only for his own sins but for those of all his forebears, including Adam.

"On Sundays, after Mass," historian Jules Michelet wrote, "the sick came in scores, crying for help,—and words were all they got: 'You have sinned, and God is afflicting you. Thank Him; you will suffer so much the less torment in the life to come. Endure, suffer, die. Has not the Church its prayers for the dead?' "[10]

Not once through the Dark Ages was Western man allowed respite from the now-rigid conviction that pain and suffering were punishment for sin. Everything that could not be explained otherwise was dumped into this single repository. Man paid a heavy price for his abysmal ignorance, and, paradoxically, the only cathartic relief for his fear and superstition was man-made: the public execution as spectacle. As Huizinga taught us in *The Waning of the Middle Ages*, "The cruel excitement and coarse compassion raised by an execution formed an important item in the spiritual food of the common people. They [the executions] were spectacular plays with a moral. [Sinners will be punished.]"[11]

The public execution was punishment for heresy or for crime. Torture almost always preceded the execution, and it rather quickly became a highly ritualized technique. The specifications for effective torture were that "it must produce a certain degree of pain, which may be measured exactly, or at least calculated, compared and hierarchized; . . . the production of pain is regulated . . . the duration of the death agony [is calculated] . . . (the court decides whether the criminal is to be strangled at once or allowed to die slowly, and the points at which this gesture of pity must occur)."[12]

Torture was never uncontrolled vengeance. Death-torture, Foucault tells us, was "the art of maintaining life in pain, by subdividing it into a 'thousand deaths,' by achieving before life ceases 'the most exquisite agonies.' "[13] All this because pain was the obvious punishment for crime and for sin. In a sense, judicial torture was the dramatization of hell and, in cases of heresy, where the goal was recantation and salvation of the soul, "the pains here . . . may also be counted as penitence and so alleviate the punishments of the beyond."[14]

When John Calvin exhorted his followers never to be weakened by pain or suffering because "God proves the faith of his people in these days by various trials," he simply reinforced the ideas of prior centuries in the new religious language of the Reformation. Calvin emphasized the penitential aspect of duress —the Christian must expect nothing but to bear a cross perpetually without complaint; the test of his faith was meek endurance of all agony and woe.[15]

We smile at the strictures now, but the truth of the matter is that Calvinistic theology still underlies our attitude toward pain, and never more so than in our reaction to cancer. The idea that cancer is punishment for sin is not a vagrant thought that flicks through the mind and disappears, but a solid belief. From my reader mail and the psychosocial literature on cancer patients, I suspect that most Americans believe, consciously or unconsciously, that cancer strikes as direct retribution for transgression, and that it must be suffered. If we understand such fundamentalism, we can also begin to understand our national incredulity at statistical evidence showing that almost half of all cancer patients die without pain.

Indeed, American attitudes toward pain and suffering are confused and incredibly naive. Although we do not admit it, most of us feel that, by sheer will power and faith, we can overcome a disease and not even feel its pain. We Americans have always believed in self-reliance, sure that with gumption and will power we could overcome any obstacle—tame the frontier, win any war, rise from rags to riches, conquer disease. This is the bootstrap philosophy William James delineated as "mind-cure optimism."[16]

Mind-cure optimism has its roots in Lutheran and Methodist theology. The believer asks: "What shall I do to be saved?" The Lutheran and Methodist answer is: "You are saved now if you would but believe it." Sheer faith can create optimism; enough will power can enable one to achieve any wanted victory. The problem with this philosophy is that, when pitted against a terminal disease of biological origin, it founders.

Most of us can cope with a certain amount of pain. Relaxation techniques (such as hypnosis, self-hypnosis, and biofeedback) and subcutaneous stimulators for muscle spasms are remarkably effective aids to control of pain. But when cancer permeates bone, presses on a nerve, or blocks a hollow organ, pain becomes excruciating, and no amount of stoicism will relieve it. Nor should it be expected to.

Anesthesiologists, oncologists, pharmacologists, and other specialists concerned with the chronic pain of advanced cancer know how to mitigate relentless pain. Unlike their many colleagues who have been described as "pharmacological calvinists,"[17] they use narcotic drugs, yet their patients do not become drug addicts. Fear of causing addiction, voiced by far too many doctors in other specialties who are caring for cancer patients, is largely the result of the deeply held religious beliefs and mind-cure optimism ingrained in our culture.

Doctors who cannot bring themselves to give adequate pain relief are like the doctors and clergymen of the last century who excoriated the physicians who invented and used anesthesia to eliminate pain during tooth extraction, surgery, and childbirth. In the early 1840s, against a common background of American and British hellfire-and-damnation revivalism, William E. Clarke, of Rochester, New York, and Crawford W. Long, of Jefferson, Georgia, independently began using ether in dental and surgical operations.

Five years later (1847), Dr. Long and Sir James Young Simpson, a professor of obstetrics at the University of Glasgow, Scotland, again without knowledge of each other's work, began using ether to prevent the pain of childbirth.

Dr. Simpson was not satisfied with the side effects of ether and turned to chloroform. He quickly published his findings, and the Scottish Calvinist clergy roared: pain, especially the pain of childbirth, was the lot of humanity; it would be a sacrilege to prevent it. "Chloroform is a decoy of Satan," one clergyman thundered, "apparently offering itself to bless women; but . . . it will . . . rob God of the deep, earnest cries which arise in time of trouble for help."[18]

The tirade against anesthesia becomes even more intriguing when you realize that potions and drugs such as opium, hashish, alcohol, mandrake, and henebane date back at least to the ancient Babylonians and, when available, were used continuously through the Middle Ages and Elizabethan England by kings and aristocrats.

Unlike exotic drugs and potions, modern anesthesia had the authority of the new science of chemistry behind it, and by the 1840s chemistry had the potential to make anesthesia available to the masses. But if everyone could be rendered unconscious by anesthesia—and therefore unaware of pain—who could pay the price of his sin? The opposition to anesthesia raged until 1853, when Queen Victoria, using the full power and authority of the crown, accepted chloroform from her physician during the birth of Prince Leopold. The Queen used it again when she was delivered of Princess Beatrice, in 1857.

Scientific anesthesia allowed the advancement of surgery, for which both doctors and patients can be grateful. Yet, despite the acknowledged practicality of anesthesia and its apparent acceptance, the semiconscious belief persists that total relief of pain stemming from nonsurgical causes is somehow immoral. Hence our admiration for endurance through suffering, instead of outrage that the suffering is allowed. Just listen to us: *"He was so brave, though in so much pain."* . . . *"She only once let us know how terrible her pain was."*

Nurses are unstinting in their admiration of burn and cancer patients who endure their pain stoically. Yet, if you ask them why their cancer patients aren't getting adequate narcotic relief, you get a predictable party-line answer: fear of creating drug addiction.

I listen in dismay. For, in all good conscience, otherwise excellent nurses are simply parroting a lesson learned in nursing school. It never occurs to them to challenge it. Their sole question is whether, in the last few weeks of a patient's life, it is morally right to administer the stepped-up narcotics finally ordered by a doctor because a patient "has suffered enough." I have never heard a nurse ask, "Why do our patients have to suffer at all?" I have never heard anyone question the self-appointed authority of the doctor who alone judges whether a helpless individual has "suffered enough."

Pain that overwhelms, not in waves but continuously, without letup, is entirely different from pain healthy people have experienced. The pain of a badly shattered bone, immediate postoperative pain, and severe pain from kidney stones are all acute and thus similar to the pain of cancer. But there is one difference: these patients are patients only temporarily—they know their pain is linear and will diminish and then end.

That is entirely different from having to suffer the pain of advanced cancer, for that pain is not only a constant reminder that death lies ahead but brings with it the certainty of intensification before death sets one free. In this sense, pain is the equivalent of torture, all-consuming and indescribably cruel.

A hospitalized cancer patient who constantly screams against excruciating pain will be abandoned—first by his doctor, who has not addressed the problem of pain with adequate medication, then by his nurses, who reinforce societal prejudices about pain, and lastly by his family, because they cannot endure any more bedside waiting for death to bring release. The abandonment of patients under these circumstances is so well documented in the massive literature on thanatology[19] (more than four thousand book titles alone) that it needs no further amplification here.

A new awareness of our inhumanity to the dying (especially cancer patients whose dying is generally quite prolonged) led to the rise of three movements dedicated to a new concern for human beings at the end of their lives.[20] The first of these movements is hospice. In the 1960s, England's Cicely Saunders, who holds degrees in nursing, social work, and medicine, and who is now Dame Cicely Saunders, led the way in creating the idea of hospice as a place and a way of humane care for dying individuals.

Based on the initial concept of hospice as a place of refuge for travelers, Dr. Saunders and a group of equally dedicated

British physicians, clergymen, nurses, social workers, and volunteers, conceived and built St. Christopher's Hospice in London. St. Christopher's embodies the new meaning of hospice, a compassionate philosophy that puts a dying individual's human dignity, rights, and sense of completion ahead of all other considerations.

This philosophy, embraced by all hospice personnel, enables a hospice team to create, for an individual dying either at home or in a hospice facility, the security that comes from knowing that one's pain will be controlled, that one's basic dignity as an individual will be maintained, that dying will not be a wretched procedure in which the tubes of medical technology protrude from every body orifice.

Hospice staffs and volunteers understand that dying individuals "need life around them, spiritual and emotional comfort . . . 'unsanitary' things like a favorite dog lying on the foot of the bed. They need their own clothes, their own pictures . . . surroundings that are familiar . . . people they know and love, people they can trust to care about them. Hospices can provide this, in . . . inpatient units [and through home-care programs]. . . . It is much better for it to happen at home."[21]

The humanity inherent in the British hospice movement fanned the American public interest in death and dying (an interest so strong that some misguided romantics nearly made it a cult). "I want to help the dying," some of the misguided would write to me after my column began appearing in their newspapers. Floating between the lines I could see their sentimental images of Walt Whitman in the hospitals of our Civil War and Florence Nightingale in the Crimea. Still, the hospice movement grew, because people were reading Dr. Elisabeth Kübler-Ross and were horrified at the bleak ending of life in a general hospital, British-, Canadian-, and American-style.

The second movement, the study of pain per se, began sporadically at medical teaching centers, where it was spearheaded by anesthesiologists. The grand old man of the movement is Dr. John Bonica, head of the Anesthesiology Department at the University of Washington Medical Center, where he founded and became the director of the Pain Clinic. Dr. Bonica's interest in the relief of chronic pain (cancer pain, for example) spurred him, in 1974, to establish the International Association for the Study of Pain. Regional chapters in this country followed, as did pain clinics and scattered CME (Continuing Medical Education) seminars on pain and ways to treat it.

Helen Neal's *The Politics of Pain*,[22] provides an excellent overview of this still-small movement and documents the uphill battle it and the rest of us face in trying to change society's congealed cultural attitudes toward relief of chronic pain. *The Politics of Pain* is a scathing indictment of the federal government's indifference to pain (the National Cancer Institute did not begin to award grants for research into cancer-pain control until October, 1979) and the "fatalistic" attitudes toward pain of a majority of doctors. Some of Ms. Neal's material is just heartbreaking, especially the unnecessary suffering inflicted on children who have cancer and adults who are dying of cancer.

The study of pain has revealed three different kinds of pain:

1. acute pain, as after surgery or injury;
2. chronic pain, as in low back pain or diseases, such as rheumatoid arthritis,[23] unfortunately labeled "benign pain";
3. cancer pain, which is chronic and often acute as well, and, further, is inextricably linked to intimate knowledge of approaching death.

"Doctors," says Dr. Edward Viner in *Over Fifty-Five*, "fail to understand the difference between acute pain, which is usually short-lived, reversible and without significant psychological implications, and the chronic pain of the cancer patient. In the latter, the physical pain is compounded by anxiety, depression, insomnia, financial and family concerns. The terminal patient cannot escape his own thoughts and the preoccupation he has with death. . . . Following hospice precepts, the physician should feel secure in giving narcotics in whatever doses are necessary, and as often as is necessary. He must become knowledgeable in the supplementary use of non-narcotic drugs such as tranquilizers, sedatives and antidepressants, to potentiate the narcotics without . . . excessive depression of the patient's ability to think and communicate."[24]

Dr. Viner was a thirty-six-year-old hematologist-oncologist at Pennsylvania Hospital, Philadelphia, when a routine physical examination revealed he had an enlarged liver. After tests, surgery for an expected malignant hepatoma was ordered. The tumor was found to be benign, but "myriad postoperative complications developed," including bloodstream infection, a series of pneumothoracies (lung ruptures), the need for more surgery, four months of hospitalization, and three months of recuperating at home.

If ever a physician was given the chance to understand the overwhelming feelings of helpless patients who are in excruciating pain and facing death, Edward Viner was. In *Over Fifty-Five,* he says frankly: "I was privileged to learn a number of indelible lessons which until then I had thought were all self-evident. First of all, while it is incompatible with our self-image of empathetic, caring people, we doctors really have no true concept of that which we ask our patients to endure physically and emotionally, all at the time when they are most vulnerable physically and emotionally. . . . In the end, my experience taught me that death is not always an enemy and that, indeed, it may well be preferable to a life of pain without dignity and without hope."[25]

Individuals whose insights are deepened enormously by personal crises often go on to make significant contributions to the expansion of knowledge in their own fields. Still, the growing body of knowledge about cancer pain in all its ramifications is bottled up in hospices and cancer centers, and fails to reach the majority of doctors, nurses, administrators of general hospitals and nursing homes, or the public.

The third movement is the rise of advocacy organizations determined to eliminate or effectively challenge deathbed pain. Some of these organizations have controversial goals, such as the legalization of active euthanasia. Others seek the legalization of passive euthanasia. Still others press for federal and state adoption of living wills, legal documents that allow competent individuals to direct their physicians and hospital or nursing-home staffs not to take "heroic" measures to prolong their lives if they are institutionalized as terminally ill. Ten states have passed such legislation,[26] but no living will has yet been challenged in court in any state; hence its legal effectiveness is uncertain.

The National Committee on the Treatment of Intractable Pain has as its prime goal the "transfer of heroin from Schedule I of the [federal government] Controlled Substances Act, which designates it of no medical use, to Schedule II, which places it in the same restricted category as morphine."[27] The NCTIP bases its case on the experience of thirty-eight countries (including those of Great Britain) which allow their physicians to use heroin when morphine cannot control pain as well as heroin can. The medicinal use of heroin to relieve the pain of dying cancer patients in this country has also been endorsed by the American Cancer Society, the American Psychiatric Society, and a few state medical societies.

One/Fourth, The Alliance For Cancer Patients And Their Families, not only specifies in its statement of purpose (see Appendix B) "the right of each patient to skillful and unstinting pain relief," but is undertaking, as its first major project, national dissemination of information about modern methods of pain relief. We who are the founders of One/Fourth (physicians, lawyers, business men and women, and myself) have studied the medical literature of cancer-pain management. Some of our board members are medical pain specialists. We know that across this country there are physicians who will welcome and use greater knowledge of cancer-pain management. We believe we can also affect the curricula of medical schools so that courses in cancer pain management become part of the curricula. We believe that an informed public will be able to make distinctions between narcotic abuse and adequate narcotic use by physicians for relief of pain. We have the confidence of all crusaders that our efforts will be a major contribution to man's centuries-old search for full relief of pain and that our efforts will someday end not only the fear of intractable cancer pain but that pain itself.

With John Merrill, I have the security of a physician who is opposed to unnecessary pain; who says, "You don't get any merit badges for suffering pain"; and who urges his patients to take their medication on a constant, timed schedule to prevent the recurrence of pain.

Every cancer patient has the right to ask his doctor, "How do you handle your patients' pain? What drugs will you use with me if I have pain that becomes intolerable? Do you prescribe drugs on a *prn* basis or a timed schedule?" Although doctors are not accustomed to such questions from patients, they are obliged to give specific answers. If a doctor gives vague or evasive answers, that is a good time to realize he is not the right doctor for you.

The right doctor is the one who knows how to control cancer pain and therefore can be optimistic and reassuring. Specific answers to the questions above will provide useful information and guard against the vague reassurance, "Don't worry, if you need pain medication, you'll get it." This promise is acceptable only when a patient and his doctor have achieved a relationship of unquestionable trust.

I realize as I write this that certain families and friends are even now watching someone they love suffer intense pain. You must ask the doctor to consult a pain specialist. If the doctor is offended by this request, respectfully hold your ground. You are paying for his services; express your willingness to pay the consultation fee. Or you can take your dear one to the nearest hospital with a cancer center. Or phone your local city health agency to learn if a hospice exists in your area and if it can offer the physical comfort and care so badly needed.

Patients slowly dying of advanced cancer in hospitals or in hospice programs where pain control is first-rate do not die in excruciating pain. Their pain is controlled, their minds are clear, their respiratory systems are only slightly depressed. Their families and friends are amazed—and so are they. Can dying of cancer really be this pain-free? It can.

Very advanced cancer (also called terminal cancer) is the stage of cancer where treatment no longer can halt or reverse the course of the disease. Metastases have begun to destroy bone, brain, or vital organs. This period may last for weeks or months, but it is the beginning of dying and, though he may never discuss it, every cancer patient who enters this phase knows it. Good treatment at this time is palliative, comforting, loving, helping, and brings to a dying individual the reassurance of good closure: what he needed to do before dying, he has done.

In the last few days of life, cancer patients are very weak, because any remaining physiological reserves are being channeled into maintenance of vital processes—blood circulation and respiration. When those processes can no longer be sustained, brain death occurs, consciousness is lost, and death is peaceful and infinitely quiet.

Part 3
RELATIONSHIPS

9.

Risk-Taking

"People don't want to talk about your cancer.
They're afraid of making a mistake. They're
afraid of getting too involved."
A young man I interviewed

A new cancer patient leaves the hospital assuming that nothing
but himself has changed. Instead, he discovers that all his
relationships with others have been subtly or overtly transformed
by the fact of his cancer. The easy familiarity, the casual give-and-
take that were part of his daily life have disappeared in a welter of
timidity, anxiety, and tension. His children rush to greet him but
in hugging him cause physical pain. He winces, tastes vomit, and
draws back. That involuntary act of self-protection becomes his
first intimation of the gulf that now separates them. He's been to
the brink, and he feels he is still clinging to the precipice. He has
no idea how to reenter the world he left behind.

His wife, calm while he was hospitalized, now is uneasy and
insecure. His parents arrive and hover nervously. Though he
managed to dress in the hospital with his wife's help, undressing is
a monumental task. He hurts all over; his head feels compressed;
his hands tremble; he hears his wife speaking, but he can't sort out
the words; he sinks into his pillow and is instantly asleep.

While he sleeps, the members of his family try to organize

themselves for the new experience of having the head of the household home ill with a disease so threatening that it will always dominate their lives. They now assume a tremendous new responsibility—the care of a cancer patient. What is expected of them? What are the right things to do? What must be avoided? What was it the doctor said? What last suggestions did the nurse make? Will this man they all love want to talk about his disease and his feelings about it? Will that be good for him or bad for him? Is he going to die? Did his doctor tell the truth when he told the family what to expect? A basic theme, *I don't want to do anything wrong,* plays endlessly in the backs of their minds.

A new cancer patient is rarely aware of his family's agonizing. Usually he is preoccupied, if not obsessed, with his own horror, resentment, and anger at what has been done to him; his fear of imminent death; his sense of defeat; his despair. Now, on top of all this, his family is self-conscious. They all but walk tippy-toe in their eagerness to be helpful, but to him their efforts reverberate as if a herd of elephants were crashing about.

In the weeks that follow, a wish is born of tension and despair. The wish is so desperate that it becomes a fantasy. The cancer patient and his family pray to be moved back in time, back to the idyllic time, the perfect life they lived before cancer invaded their home.

Never mind that they in fact were a family very much at odds with each other, or a family with no strong feelings for each other. In the rosy haze of retrospect, their prior life seems orderly and good. Now, like the bathroom that is a clutter of medicines, syringes, and pressure packs, life is disorderly, distasteful, and grim.

Even when a family is sound and happy, cancer makes incessant demands on their time, their compassion, their private lives. In fact, in a family where people really care about each other—where love, acceptance, and understanding are present—cancer will consume them all the more, precisely because of their concern for the one who has the disease.

Cancer in a child undermines a loving mother's devotion to her other children; the child with cancer has to come first. When it is the mother who has cancer, her children (even if adults) are terrified: Mother may die and leave them unprotected and alone. A wife's cancer doubles the number of responsibilities a husband has to assume, and it creates in the wife an enormous extra burden of guilt. When a husband and father, the family breadwinner, has cancer, his anger and frustration are compounded by fears of job loss and the very real possibility that he may no longer be hireable at all. An adolescent who has cancer may be in the sorriest position of all: his future, almost within his grasp, may never be his.

Except in a few instances where hospitals have created outreach programs for newly discharged cancer patients, home-care programs are almost nonexistent; cancer patients and their families are expected to do the best they can, on their own. With no blueprints and no outside professional help, families somehow muddle through. But the days are long and anxious; the nights are lonely and anguished; hope falters, despair intrudes. The painful task of inching through each day obscures the goal of getting well again and squelches hope.

I sometimes think of the similarities between new cancer patients and their families and those pioneering families who pushed west alone, into uncharted wilderness, for the sake of a goal that became increasingly difficult to recall. The perils are similar: ever-present threat of death; seemingly endless, frequently painful journeying; a host of fears that may or may not be realized; desperate effort simply to get through each day; and yet, from a marvel of inner strength, the ability to live with unforeseen risks and, somehow, take them in stride.

With cancer, risk-taking is not foolhardy courage; it is choosing to live as fully as possible despite the disease:

The cancer patient who is disfigured by cancer treatment yet refuses to accept second-class status is a risk-taker.

The adolescent who loses a leg to osteosarcoma but then learns to ski is a risk-taker.

The woman who has endured the horrible feelings of shame that are a consequence of mastectomy and bravely says to her mate, "I want us to make love again," takes a huge risk.

And her husband, who has mixed feelings about this first postsurgical intimacy yet tenderly gathers her into his arms and trusts his instincts, takes an almost equal risk.

Every physician who is honest with his patients—honest about diagnosis and prognosis, honest about his inability to predict their life span,[1] honest about the options and hazards of treatment, honest enough to refer that patient to another physician, if he finds himself unable to be sympathetic—takes risks.

Families become risk-takers when they restrain themselves from making decisions for the member of the family who has cancer, and when they recognize that adult advice in decision-making is one thing, but frightened attempts at manipulation are quite another.

Parents become risk-takers when they allow their child who has cancer to make his own mistakes and when they protest the discrimination against this child (and his siblings) that the community may inflict.

Friends become risk-takers when they make the initial visit to a new cancer patient and walk into his room without knowing what they will find, or what to say or do.

Foremen, heads of small firms, executives of corporations who, despite mixed feelings, phone to say, "We want you back; we'll need to talk about how much work you can handle," are risk-takers.

Any family member becomes a risk-taker when he faces up to the reality that cancer has come to the family, and that the experience of it will not vanish. He maintains that status when he quietly refuses the follies so often thrust on him by well-meaning relatives and neighbors: all the newspaper clippings about "breakthroughs" and "miracle" cures; all the mindless notions about wheatgrass diets, or coffee enemas as part of detoxification programs[2]; all the worthless articles about obscure cancer "clinics" where doctors scorned by the medical establishment and the National Cancer Institute are "restoring" dying patients to glowing life. Here a family member risks the hurt feelings and disappointment of others, their hostility, their turning away. But he must take these risks if he is to keep his sanity and not become mired in wishful thinking and unreality.

If we cancer patients are to control our own lives, we too must take risks. At the start of our experience with cancer, our scale of values is so cockeyed that every protest on our own behalf seems an enormous risk. Which of us has the nerve to tell a well-meaning friend that little gems of folk philosophy such as, "After all, dear, we're all terminal,"[3] are not helpful but infuriatingly naive? How many of us have the courage to ask our doctors why they are doing this, recommending that, ignoring such and such? Which of us will risk our physician's irritation for the sake of learning what we need to know about our disease? How many of us who feel rejected by friends will take the risk of phoning those who stay away, in order to make sure the thread is not broken? Some friends and relatives have terrible fantasies about us and our cancer. Have we the courage to renegotiate these friendships by helping them get over their fears?

Tom Snyder, interviewing me on the *Tomorrow* show[4] shortly after my column began running in the *Chicago Daily News,* was gentle and truly interested in what I was trying to accomplish with the column. After some twenty minutes he suddenly leaned forward and asked his most important question:

TS: Why is it so uncomfortable to talk about cancer? I mean, I'm really uncomfortable, Jory, talking about cancer.
JG: Are you, really?
TS: Yeah, I've been uncomfortable all through this thing. I mean, the guys are standing here, it is so quiet in here, you can hear the ratings dropping. You know, we're not talking, we're not joking, we're not smoking.
JG: Do you really think our ratings are dropping?
TS: No, no. That's a little joke—"hey, it's so quiet in here you can hear the ratings dropping."
JG: They're not dropping. They're going up right now. . . . It's quiet because this discussion reminds everyone of his own mortality. There's something unreal about

talking with a woman who says, "I'm going to die of this thing some day." That's enough to make anyone uncomfortable—it makes *me* uncomfortable thinking about it. But you know, Mr. Snyder, if I can sit here talking about it, you can sit here and listen. And you're doing just fine. . . . [5]

I still admire Tom Snyder for his honesty that night on network television. He wanted to understand what was bothering him, and he had the courage to explore his own feelings. Few talk-show hosts feel comfortable interviewing people who are mortally wounded. After all, what do you say to someone who is trying to face his own death? How can you possibly discuss that calmly? If you start with a topic as grim as death, how do you escape its horrid fascination and go on to talk about something else?

Friends who learn we have cancer are in the same position. But where the talk-show host knows that he'll be off the air in a few minutes, our friends may well feel that they will never be able to change the subject. What if we are obsessed with death? What if we stare at them and turn our heads away? My God, if all this is in the back of their minds, what courage must be summoned to come to us again.

When death is personified in us, those who know us or love us or work with us are sharply reminded of their own mortality. If we can get cancer, so can they. If we must suffer and die before our lives are complete, so may they. For some, this is just too much to handle. They close the door on it and us.

You and I who have cancer weep often enough over the threat to our lives and all we hold dear. The image our family and friends cannot shake is that we are dying and leaving them behind with their grief and excruciating sense of loss. Frightened and equally forlorn as we, they decide to hide their feelings from us—and blunder right into the kind of silence we are most likely to misinterpret. Or they say only what they think we should hear. In either case, the gulf between us widens because no one has the courage to talk about his sense of impending loss.

The most remarkable statement ever made to me by a friend upon hearing from me that I had cancer was "Jory, that's a tragedy." He was stunned by my news, but he managed to speak from his heart. I was then, and still am, grateful for those few words. They acknowledged the threat to my life and also said that my life mattered. I have described this incident often, it was that important to me. But a reporter interviewing me once said he did not feel "That's a tragedy" would be of help to everyone who has cancer. I said that I wasn't thinking of an all-purpose statement, that an all-purpose statement would become as banal as "Have a good day."

The friend who understands my strained emotions when I tell him I have cancer may only say, "Oh, Jory." But if he reaches for my hand or puts his arm around me, he is at that moment doing enough.

The friend who quietly asks, "Care to tell me a little more?" is willing to hear, and he too is doing enough for the moment.

The friend whose tears are visible lets me know he is prepared to share sadness.

Risk-takers, all.

Often, the risks are tremendous. Here is a letter from one of my readers asking for help with a not-uncommon and tragic problem. Solving it demands tremendous willingness on the part of the cancer patient and his family (especially the family member who wrote to me) to take risks.

Dear Jory:

My father has come home from the hospital totally depressed. His prognosis is good, but he has undergone a radical personality change. Before cancer, he was an affable man, though low-key and not very demonstrative. But now he has become a withdrawn stranger who sits gazing at nothing for hours. He cannot be reached, even by my mother's tenderest love. His silence is destroying the family, because my brothers and sisters (all married) feel he should never have learned his diagnosis—look what it's done to him. Have you any suggestions?

I had several; the one with the greatest potential involved the greatest risk:

> You may be able to help your father break through his depression by sitting with him quietly and finally saying, "You never complain, but it must be terrible." This may allow your father to open up and confide, "It's worse than terrible." Then you can ask another question, "How much worse?" If your father begins enumerating woes, say nothing, just listen. Your goal is to help him express at least some of the anger that is submerged under his depression. Right now, he's desperately trying to be stoic and uncomplaining, but his decision to be so makes him feel worse.
>
> I realize that we are all afraid to acknowledge anger, for fear it will become uncontrollable rage. But the risk is worth taking because any anger over having cancer is legitimate, and it needs to be expressed not once but many times. Will you be able to listen to anger without feeling you must participate? The anger of those we love can make us feel very defensive, even though their anger is fundamentally at the disease.

Another of my readers confides her fears about maintaining a long-standing friendship with a woman who has disfiguring cancer:

> We have never been physically close. A light peck on the cheek after a long vacation was our limit; we have expressed our warmth in other ways. . . . Fortunately, I had just read your column about showing affection for friends who are ill. All my instincts responded to your suggestion to put my arms around my friend when I went to visit, but I didn't really know if I could, especially in view of our previous reserve. Somehow, as we greeted each other, I knew it was the thing to do, and I took her into my arms immediately. She clung to me—what comfort that was for both of us. . . . I feel that by letting down the bars, expressing my feelings spontaneously and sincerely, it brought my dear friend and me closer. Bless you. . . .

I have so much admiration for this reader, for her willingness to risk herself in a human encounter that she could easily have restricted to something less than the rich experience it became. To recognize one's own vulnerability but proceed regardless, in order to keep the human situation going, is risk-taking of the highest order. How remarkable that it almost always evokes its own rewards.

10.

Sex, Love, and Cancer

"Dear Jory,
   Thank you for answering my letter. . . . I always thought I was the only one who had this problem."
A column reader

For me, Easter and Thanksgiving of 1975 did not mark the joy of resurrection or the celebration of living but the destruction of my feelings about myself as a woman. On Good Friday, I had my first mastectomy, and on the day before Thanksgiving, my second. The impact on me was devastating and almost indescribable—horror that would not lessen, a feeling of utter worthlessness, and enormous disgust. Somebody told me of Alice Roosevelt Longworth's description of herself after becoming a "bilateral," as the women who fitted me for prostheses now referred to me. Alice Roosevelt Longworth had said, "I feel like a plucked chicken," a phrase so accurate that I cringed each time it came to mind.

   In desperation, I turned to the two resources that had steadied me through other catastrophes—the wise and compassionate physician who had been my psychoanalyst, and my writing. I began seeing my psychoanalyst, Dr. Max Forman, again, and I accepted a newspaper syndicate commission to write a series of articles on ways of overcoming the grief of mastectomy.

Since I really had no idea how to resolve my own sense of loss, the writing went badly: weeks of false starts during which I typed pitiful or angry expressions of my own pain. Twice I had to ask for deadline extensions; finally, the deadline could be extended no longer, and somehow, because I had to, I began to dredge from an exhausted part of my brain and my heart some focus and control.

"To discover you have cancer is to discover fear," I wrote. "But with breast cancer, fear has unholy dimensions, because treatment means mutilation, an assault on your womanhood, your body image, your very being. Maybe you are able to ask your surgeon rational questions: How long will I be away from work? from home? from whatever? But all the careful answers are lost in the thunder of a demoniac symphony—howling strings, screeching clarinets and horns, booming tympani. Your world crashes in."[1]

Any surgical procedure that will forever alter a part of ourselves is as terrifying as the disease it is supposed to "cure." Other types of surgery are also terrifying, but at least they are restorative; an end, say, to ulcers. But surgery that will destroy our sense of wholeness is almost beyond acceptance. Though surgeons honestly believe their own words when they tell us that *none* of their other patients has had the problems we have in "adjusting" to identical surgery,[2] their words are hollow. Unless they themselves have undergone such an experience, they have no real comprehension of it. If they had been there before us, they would speak quite differently.

We cannot fault doctors for wanting to believe that what they have done to us in the attempt to halt malignancy will not matter that much since we still have our lives. But too many doctors leave us sinking in a tumultuous sea of feelings that we cannot even express. Desperate for a compassionate phrase, a nonintimidating question that will enable us to stammer out some of our pain and despair, we hear only the sterile, "You must think positively," advice that is as useful as a candy lifesaver would be to a drowning man.

If you examine the curricula of medical schools and hospital

residency programs, and the courses in continuing medical education, you find most of them oddly behind the times. The emphasis
is almost entirely on technical knowledge of the human body, its
ills (including the diseases that assault, derange, and destroy
anatomic function), and their treatment. But just as the treatment
of chronic cancer pain is rarely taught, so the impact of cancer on
the human psyche and human sexuality is mainly ignored.

Thus, a highly respected physician, a professor of gynecology
and obstetrics at a major university teaching hospital, could say as
recently as 1977, in a new textbook of gynecology and obstetrics,
that the "proper treatment [for cancer of the vulva] although
disfiguring, is not mutilative. Women can lead normal lives after a
radical vulvectomy and node dissection. In the rare young woman
with this disease, sexual activity, orgasm, and even childbirth are
possible. Counseling before and support after treatment are
important."[3]

Not mutilative? The ritual circumcision of women practiced
in Africa and South America, which the Western world regards
with horror, consists of removal of the labia minora and the
clitoris. Yet the same physician defines a radical vulvectomy as
"removal of the entire vulva, including the labia majora, labia
minora, hymenal remnants, and clitoris. The lateral incision is at
the labiocrural fold; superiorly, the mons pubis is removed;
inferiorly, the perineum is incised near the anus; and the medical
incisions usually lie just outside the level of the urethral meatus.
Of course, the limits of the vulvectomy must be outside the tumor
margins, and each case must be individualized. The distal one half
of the urethra can be removed without loss of continence. The
skin of the anterior aspect of the anus can be sacrificed. Rarely is it
necessary to remove the bladder and/or rectum."[4]

It is hard to read this contribution to medical knowledge
without becoming incensed. The author is playing with words
when he says that the procedure is not mutilative. It is massive
amputation, but if it can be successfully denied through word-
magic, then the physician can dismiss the intensity of his patient's
grief when she weeps over what has been done to her. His careful

surgery has extended her life, and, according to the textbooks, it is "not mutilative."

But, even when doctors are sensitive to a surgically humiliated cancer patient's plight, they are disadvantaged in not really knowing how to help. Until the last few years, medical textbooks have not paid any attention to the effects of common diseases, let alone mutilative surgery, on human sexuality. "Physicians are aware that the valuation of sexuality in our culture has undergone, and is still undergoing, a change," Dr. Alex Comfort tells us in his introduction to *Sexual Consequences of Disability*.[5] "This change," he says, "is less a *sexual revolution* in the behavioral sense than a general increase in frankness and expectation. . . . [Patients now ask,] 'Will it [radical surgery or other treatment] affect my sex life?' . . . With the recognition that sexual function is normally life!ong, needlessly . . . compromising intercourse has become proper grounds for a malpractice suit. . . .

"The negative attitude of most persons toward the disabled, the unconscious castration anxieties which disability or deformity excite, and the real social problems of sexual expression in isolated or institutionalized people are often dealt with by projection: the sexual needs of such people are better minimized or ignored, rather than discussed, for fear of embarrassing them—by which we mean that they embarrass or disturb *us*. Their sexual needs attract the same disapproval we accord to the sexual needs of older persons, as though they were in some way unseemly."

Here and there at rehabilitation centers in the early 1970s, doctors of physical medicine, treating (among others) some of this country's mainly young, mainly male, 120,000-plus paraplegics and quadriplegics, began coming to grips with their patients' needs for affirmation of sexuality. As awareness grew, so did the recognition that just as disability changes the way satisfaction of needs will now be accomplished, so it also heightens the need to feel wanted and loved. "The notion that serious illness eliminates sexual interest is untenable," Lilian Lieber wrote as principal investigator in a revealing hospital study of affection between patients with advanced cancer and their spouses.[6]

When two physicians and a technical consultant at the University of Minnesota's Program in Human Sexuality published *Sexual Options for Paraplegics and Quadriplegics,*[7] with explicit black-and-white photography illustrating sexual options and a text that sanctioned the right to be sexual, Little, Brown, the publishers, discovered they had a best-seller.

Unfortunately, these messages of human need for sexual expression despite cancer and because of cancer have failed to reach doctors and other health professionals who treat cancer patients. From nurses and social workers in pediatric oncology units who feel compelled to destroy the few snatched minutes of privacy two adolescent patients of the opposite sex create for themselves within the hospital, to the directors of the Connecticut Hospice, who in 1976 released plans for construction of a hospice building with beds for forty-four terminal patients but only four private rooms, it is evident that cultural attitudes about the legitimacy of sexuality in cancer patients are, if not vastly disapproving, vastly ignorant of human needs.

"I believe in four-bedded rooms," Dr. Sylvia Lack, the medical director of the Connecticut Hospice, told Joan Kron in an interview for *New York* magazine,[8] "to get peer support from people experiencing the same problems." When Ms. Kron spoke with hospital consultant John Thompson about this lack of privacy, he said, "Although government regulations generally call for 60 percent single-bedded rooms in all new hospitals, Hospice will have 90 percent four-bedded rooms. . . . Interaction of staff, patient, and family is the key to Hospice's programs, but with private rooms, you can't interact."[9]

Long before I began writing this chapter, I instigated computer searches of medical and nursing literature on sexuality in cancer patients. I found little, and what I managed to locate reflected the uneasiness of the researchers rather than either compassionate understanding of human needs or straightforward help and insights for other clinicians.[10] When I wrote to participants in a few much-publicized symposia on human sexuality, asking for copies of their presentations, I was disappointed in the lack of insight in the materials I received. The "experts" mainly mouthed platitudes about sexuality in healthy persons and kept their distance from the agonizing human reality of the special problems created by radical surgery for cancer. They also kept their distance by consistently referring to individuals as "the patient."

Though sometimes the term "the patient" is unavoidable, I have always thought it remarkable that medical literature, medical teaching, and even discussions between physicians consistently rely on such impersonal terminology—"the patient," "the physician." This usage is a distancing mechanism, separating physicians from their patients so that the dangers of becoming emotionally involved are minimized. To say "my patient," or "this patient," presumes a specific individual with whom one has a specific relationship.

Any alteration of one's physical intactness is a hideous experience. Therefore, when the treatment of cancer clearly will alter a patient's sense of wholeness, a caring physician will anticipate his patient's vulnerability and realize that even though his patient does not ask directly, "What will this do to my sex life?" the question exists and must be answered. A caring physician will know that this is not the time to act like a discreet private citizen. "If he wanted to know, he'd ask," is an unworthy rationalization.

But how many doctors would know what to do if asked? How many doctors understand that the depression that follows such mutilation as the removal of the breast(s), the uterus, the voice box, the testis, part of the colon,[11] is frequently deeper than fear of cancer itself? Psychiatrists excepted, doctors are not being trained to understand depression as a phenomenon in itself,[12] and an inevitable consequence of radical, mutilative surgery. Medical journals and textbooks perpetuate such inaccuracies as, "The overwhelming majority of women who are subjected to a mastectomy accept the loss of their breast with equanimity. Occasionally, a woman has difficulty in accepting this surgical loss. . . ."[13]

Thus, Oncology Times, a monthly newspaper for cancer specialists, headlined a June, 1980, report of a study conducted by the psychiatric service at Memorial Hospital in New York City, "Depression Rare Among Cancer Patients." According to the report, the study showed that physicians at Memorial Hospital "requested a psychiatric consultation [for only] 334 patients out of the 6,735 who were admitted to the hospital during the study period." Does this mean that patients at the world's largest private cancer center[14] are rarely depressed? Or does it indicate that doctors cannot recognize depression when they see it? Or, that doctors accept depression as a normal consequence of cancer for which nothing can or should be done?

Considering how little emotional help is available to cancer patients, it is not surprising that many of us feel a constant sadness shadowing even the happy occasions we continue to celebrate. Although we are wonderfully adroit at masking it, the sadness persists, because of the daily reminders (when bathing or dressing, say, or sharing a bed) of what has been lost. It is a form of chronic depression and is precisely the area where we need help, so that we can make peace with our feelings of irretrievable loss.

Sometimes our mates write us off. More often we write ourselves off. For every man who heads straight for a divorce court after telling his wife who has had a mastectomy, "You are no longer a woman," there is a woman so bereft over her loss, so insecure, that she fails to give her caring husband a chance to help her. For every man whose wife withdraws from sexual intimacy following his ileostomy,[15] there is a husband so ashamed of the change in his body image and the extrusion of rectal wastes into a soft appliance attached to his abdominal wall, that he holds his wife at bay.

Both science and culture teach us that male and female reproductive organs are the essence of human sexuality, and that everything else is peripheral. If doctors accept this age-old precept as fact, then it is easy to understand why they do not comprehend the significance of breast loss to women. So long as science views breasts important solely for infant breast-feeding, doctors will fail to realize that, for women, breasts are important in themselves, the always-visible symbol of their womanhood. Many women, perhaps most women, equate their breasts, not their reproductive organs, with the proud triumvirate of male genitalia; to these women, breast loss has nothing to do with whether they are past their childbearing years. They mourn the destruction of their body image—that image each of us has of ourselves and others as whole and valuable or empty and permanently damaged.

This explains why most women who have suffered breast loss remain silently inconsolable long after their scars have healed. This also explains why men who are incapable of understanding their own panicky reactions to breast loss flee. The surgical cutting-off of a woman's breast is symbolic castration and arouses the deep fears of castration that all men know to varying degrees within their lifetime.

In the nineteenth and early twentieth centuries, people, and the characters in the novels[16] they read, often confessed to feelings of shame associated with the involuntary exposure of their intimate selves. This kind of shame, this experience of being unprotected,[17] naked, revealed as incongruous, has not disappeared, despite the fact that today we rarely hear anyone say, "I am ashamed of myself." It reaches its most grievous consequences when a sexual part of ourselves has been excised by a surgeon's knife. A letter from one of my readers, a middle-aged woman who has lost both breasts to surgery for cancer, makes this crystal-clear when she confesses that her deepest fear is what the undertaker will think when he someday must undress her corpse.

Because this sort of shame is virtually never discussed, each one of us who is confronted by it believes it to be unique to ourself. We assume that we are the only one to experience it and though it is not our fault, yet in some oblique, unfathomable way it is our fault. Even the mating contract has been breached: *I am no longer what you loved.*[18]

Shame of this quality is rarely understood outside the psychiatric community. It yields only to compassion and the most delicate understanding—the kind of understanding our doctors and nurses ought to have, our mates ought to have, and we, ourselves, above all, ought to have.

But because our feelings of shame are so degrading, our

unconscious mind, adroit in all painful matters, rechannels the feelings that accompany shame and sends back the message, *I am just so depressed.* And profound, excruciating depression is what our unconscious allows us to feel. Shame is not acceptable, depression is. In fact, depression is such an *expected* condition of cancer that it inevitably contributes to the way others react to us. For example: one stereotype is that our presence will be unbearable because an ominous cloud of depression hovers over us and them, exactly the way Joe Btfsplk's black cloud of bad luck in *Lil' Abner* brings catastrophe to Dogpatch.

Though depression is indeed a major part of cancer, its roots are not in the disease itself but in our deepest feelings about ourselves and what has happened to us and been done to us.

In the safe environment of my psychoanalyst's office, I found the understanding and help that allowed me to discover the roots of my depression. For more than a year, I had felt the oppressive presence of death waiting outside every room by day and standing silently by my bed each night. In dreams, I screamed against the closing of my coffin, pushed death away with my hands, fought to live. But awake, even though I was working hard, death never left me alone.

One day, once again in tears, I begged, "Max, what *is* it? Why can't I rise above this, shake it off, feel optimistic again?"

"Because you feel so ashamed," Max said quietly.

His explanation had the power of revelation: "shame" encompassed every miserable feeling I had about myself and about being breastless. I wept, of course. Acknowledging shame is excruciating, but it was a turning point for me because I suddenly understood that my endless depression and fixation on imminent death were a wholly unconscious displacement of the real problem: humiliation.

From that day on, I had a firm base upon which to begin redefining myself. I was no longer a freak in my own eyes. As I began to believe in myself once again, I learned I was still sexually desirable and that, somehow, I was allowing myself to become more feminine than before. I discovered that men still wanted to love me and protect me. In many ways, I have far more happiness now than I knew before cancer became part of my life.

I am certainly not the only cancer patient who has learned that, despite radical surgery, he or she is still intact as a person. One way or another, many of us find our ways back to full belief in our essential selves. A couple who truly love and trust and have patience with each other can achieve miracles for themselves, and the new bond is deeper, more moving to each of them, than anything they have known before.

In the most precious of all relationships, unselfish love, a confession of our agony is possible—*I feel destroyed.*

"I know, I know," the other answers, tenderly enfolding us in the deep embrace that says, *You are not destroyed for me, your wounds only make me love you more than ever.* The same healing comes from loving acceptance by a trusted parent, or from the close friend who has never once betrayed a confidence, and who can hear our grief and help restore us to ourselves.

At a few cancer centers in this country, doctors and therapists, working as a team, are providing safe conduct for cancer patients through the convoluted emotional channels that follow mutilative surgery. Unfamiliar with the phrase "safe conduct," they refer to their work as rehabilitation, but safe conduct is far more accurate.

The team I know best is headed by Dr. Andrew von Eschenbach, a young urologist, and Dorothy Rodriguez, a nurse and enterostomal therapist, at M. D. Anderson Hospital and Tumor Institute in Houston. They epitomize intelligence and sensitivity in an area that most physicians and nurses find acutely uncomfortable. In their training films for professionals, the key to the success of their programs for patients becomes apparent instantly. It is their calm, accepting attitude, which indicates, "I've heard your problem before, I understand it, and it's okay."

As editors of a new medical textbook, *Sexual Rehabilitation of The Urologic Cancer Patient,*[19] Andrew von Eschenbach and Dorothy Rodriguez provide enlightenment of a kind I have seen only in Alex Comfort's *Sexual Consequences of Disability.* Each contributed special chapters that reveal the ways they encourage discussions of sexuality with their patients. Though I would hope that no one will adopt their techniques as formulae, they are, in fact, wonderfully descriptive of ways doctors and nurses can provide frightened and discouraged cancer patients with hope and specific help.

Rereading their book, I am struck again by the help doctors and nurses could give, but for the most part do not give. And yet I know that eventually some well-meaning member of a hospital staff, or the leader of a self-help group, will misinterpret, say, my explanation of shame and will urge a cancer patient to "talk about your shame, confront it." Similar gross distortions have surfaced in other situations amateurs would best leave alone: for example, the nurse in a hospital cancer unit who had attended one course on Dr. Elisabeth Kübler-Ross's stages of dying and was overheard telling a dying patient, "There, there, I know you're in Stage Four [Depression], but I'm going to help you get to Stage Five [Acceptance]."

"Love can't be taken for granted," Dorothy Rodriguez once said to me. "Men and women do not leave their sexuality at home when they enter a hospital for cancer treatment any more than they leave their emotions at home. If anything, their needs for physical intimacy and human warmth increase; it is so important for couples to share their feelings lovingly during this time of crisis.

"A man is distressed when his mate must undergo a mastectomy. He needs to recognize that she not only will have pain and postsurgical exhaustion but is likely also to fear rejection [by him] because of her physical change. He needs to understand that all her feelings about herself as a person and a lover can be shattered by the impact of this cancer and this surgery, and that if ever his concern and tenderness are needed it is now.

"Both need to acknowledge that her breast is an important part of her body and her image of herself, but she must be reassured that her femininity and glowing personality are not dependent on the presence of a breast.

"A husband must realize that as a lover and life partner he is the brightest mirror to reflect back her beauty and value. In the hospital, he can be that mirror by helping her to walk, rubbing her back, sitting close to her, holding her hand. This is a time to share affection and tenderness. A small gift, a single rose, a card that says 'I love you' will bind a couple intimately during this time of crisis.

"No one who has just had surgery for cancer is able to take love for granted. Love must be openly expressed, so that it can serve as a beginning for the sharing of intimate feelings and thoughts. A woman who is ill and who has lost so much to cancer and its treatment needs bountiful security and strength—the man she loves is uniquely qualified to give both. At the same time, she and her doctors and nurses need to know that *he* needs strength and support to see beyond the bandages and the scars in order to focus on the person he loves and who loves him in return. Both may need time to cry, not alone, but together. The pain and hurt need not be hidden. In fact, they are ameliorated by being shared.

"More than one man who has become impotent after treatment for cancer of the bladder or prostate has felt certain his wife's love would disappear. He says to his nurses, 'I'm no good to her now. How can I start anything, if I can't finish it?' He means: 'How have I the right to do anything to arouse her when I can't have an erection and complete the act of intercourse?'

"If a man's sole concept of sexuality is penile-vaginal intercourse [and that function is destroyed by disease and treatment], he will believe intimacy is impossible, and the essential intimate relationship with his wife will be destroyed.

"At the same time his wife may be saying to herself, 'I love the kissing, the touching, the hugging, the snuggling we do; these are important to me. If he only *knew* how much warmth these give me; that he matters in so many ways that have nothing to do with [sexual] intercourse.

"She must tell him all this, because every man needs confirmation of his worth and significance as a man. For him, it is not easy, but it can be done. With a loving, helping wife, a man can regain confidence in his ability to give and receive love. I see it happen all the time.

"Even when a patient's death is impending, that patient's sexuality is an integral part of his or her personality and needs. That patient may not want or even feel capable of sexual intercourse, but his need to be loved and lovable does not diminish. Sexuality is never separated from an individual.

"A thirty-two-year-old patient of mine had extensive cancer resulting in a colostomy and a urinary diversion. On the third day, she could not restrain tears. I suggested to her husband that he sit on her bed and hold her while they wept together. I closed the door to their room and asked the staff not to disturb them. They needed to be intimate, to hold each other and share their pain."[20]

The sexuality of human beings, their ability to be creative in sex and love, far exceeds that of other animals. Cancer treatment often challenges the creativity that many couples have repressed because of a stiflingly narrow interpretation of the act of making love.

I want such couples to be reassured that lovemaking under *any* condition is not a singular experience, not a new experience, not a shameful experience. It is not experimenting for the sake of experimenting, but a shared search for the deepest expressions of human trust and love. When trust and love exist, they encompass closeness and sharing, tenderness and caring, and the spontaneity, the irresistible joy, the laughter, the pleasure, the reaffirmation of self and the other who completes self, through whatever ways two people reach each other.

Part 4
ACTS OF FAITH

11.

The Fight for Life

"The woods are lovely, dark and deep.
But I have promises to keep,
And miles to go before I sleep."
Robert Frost

Do you remember when you were a child and another child dared you to do something that was so frightening you shivered at the very thought? Then another child would double-dare you, and, since your courage and your integrity were on the line, you had to take the double-dare? Often, double-dares pushed you into some kind of nearly impossible physical action that put your life at risk or at least threatened broken bones.

As a child, I took a great many double-dares and I broke a great many bones. Ask me now, was any double-dare worth broken bones, and I might hesitate, because adult logic and intellect caution against foolhardiness. But children always need to prove themselves. And I know that sometimes proving our courage against even the most foolish, idiotic challenge is essential, if we are to learn who we are and what our capacities are.

Cancer is an extraordinary challenge, and, to meet it even halfway, I had to invent my own double-dares, and I met them as a way of rising from depression, despondency, and despair.

I'd say to myself, "You're walking badly. You aren't standing straight. You're relieving the pain in your corroded lumbars by leaning forward on your pelvis. I double-dare you to get yourself to an orthopedic surgeon and learn what exercises you can do to correct at least some of these problems." So I took my own dare, and, after months of effort, the exercises had their effect on my spine and improved my gait.

Next it was, "I double-dare you to walk home from the clinic," a distance of exactly two miles. In the beginning, I could walk only a block or two before exhaustion forced me to look for a cab. Four months later, I was able to cover more than a mile before beginning to feel the effort. By the time winter set in and I was forced to discontinue walking, I could make all but the last three blocks home without feeling I would collapse on the street.

At the end of that same summer I sometimes walked more than half a mile in a different direction, to a vacant, leveled block of city land where people were gardening. I discovered the gardeners just about the time their tomatoes were ripe, their salad vegetables green, their eggplant ready for picking, their flowers in glorious bloom. I was so envious; I had not gardened in years.

One day it occurred to me that I could do something about my envy: "I double-dare you to join them next year and plant your own plot."

"But I can't do the spading or the heavy work," I complained to myself. "I'm not even sure I can drag a hose."

The double-dare voice said, "Then find someone to garden with you." So I did that, and it was an infinitely rewarding experience.

I have had a severe flare-up every year since my cancer diagnosis. Each time, it means more pain, more treatment, heightened fear, and taut awareness of the precariousness of life. During some of these episodes, it does not seem that the disease can be brought under control; I panic and begin thinking not of life but of death. The first time this occurred, a period that lasted the better part of a year, all my energy was focused on meeting three commitments: work, daily radiation treatment, exhausted sleep. But I hardly felt I was living, I was merely hanging onto life.

Eventually, I dragged myself back to my hairdresser, because being well groomed was a matter of pride. One day he[1] said, "You need a lift. Let me turn you into a blonde." I thought he was mad, and I protested, but he would not give up. So I took the chance, and later, when I looked in the mirror and saw how a gaunt brunette, whose dark hair accentuated every hollow in her face, had been transformed into a delicate blonde, I warmed to a pleasure I had not known for months.

Thank God for a background of double-dares accepted. Like any good early training, it serves me now when it is imperative that cancer not be an excuse for refusing change or denying myself new experiences. It is terrible enough when others write us off, but catastrophic when we discount ourselves.

By any statistical standards, most people with the degree of disease I have would have succumbed long ago. Why am I still here, working harder than ever, accepting lectures across the country, leading an active life, not dying?

I live because I think I can.

I live because I am not ready to die.

I live because I passionately want to live and will not die before I must.

The fight for life is not mysterious; it is simply a rage to live. That rage is reinforced by every physician, every friend, every member of our family who also does not give up on us at the outset and who will not allow us to give up on ourselves even after recurrence.[2]

Inherent in the diagnosis of cancer is outrage that a disease, *a disease,* now will wreck every aspect of our lives. That fury should be treasured, for it leads through *why me?* to *it is me, what am I going to do about it?* and, *I'll be damned if I'll give in yet.*

Some doctors would say that I have managed to augment my own immune system.[3] This is a theory; it has not yet been proved. Max Forman and other psychoanalysts acknowledge that the fundamental will to live can be fostered and strengthened into extending life that has meaning and worth. *Extending life,* not curing the disease.

Norman Cousins, fighting a crippling collagen disease back in 1964, "knew that pain could be affected by attitudes," knew that "we are largely illiterate about pain and so are seldom able to deal with it rationally." Mr. Cousins began watching old Marx Brothers films to give himself the "anesthetic effect of genuine belly laughter," and found that ten minutes of belly laughter gave him "two hours of pain-free sleep."[4]

Mr. Cousins made a genuine comeback against overwhelming odds and years later, writing about the way he made it, in *Anatomy of an Illness,* insists that "the will to live is not a theoretical abstraction, but a physiologic reality with therapeutic characteristics."[5]

Mr. Cousins says, "Since I didn't accept the verdict" (he was told his odds were five hundred to one against recovery), "I wasn't trapped in the cycle of fear, depression and panic that frequently accompanies a supposedly incurable illness."[6] The equivocation in his word "frequently" troubles me. Nobody faces with equanimity the sudden, penetrating knowledge that his life will end. Still, I admire Mr. Cousins' courage. He simply refused to give in.

My own experience differs. I was trapped in the cycle of fear, depression, and panic, and I needed two years and incredible amounts of encouragement and help to become free. Mind you, each time my disease flares, the cycle, which has been at rest, begins its inexorable revolutions like a gigantic waterwheel, nearly drowning me in fear, depression, panic, and the seduction of death. Mr. Cousins does not mention that last, but with cancer, as with any disease for which cure is in question, it is unavoidable. For death promises a way out of the discouragement and humiliation, the helplessness, and the pain. But death is also final, the end of everything we are part of here on earth.

When we weep over our eventual death, it is because we glimpse, in moments of absolute clarity, the way life will go on without us. Everyone will be here—except us. Our families will sit down to dinner together—without us. They will gather for the traditional holidays—without us. We will not be here to share triumphs, to protect when protection is needed, or ever again to hold one another close, warm, safe.

It is we who must leave; the others will still be here together, to weep over our loss, comfort each other, and then find ways to go on sharing life and laughter. That is the mournful dirge-sadness of leave-taking, of dying, and each of us who has to face our dying knows the stabbing loneliness that wells up when we contemplate our own death.

But to wish for our own death before the disease forces it is a tragedy. Death will come, because everything that lives must die. Even stars die. Life is now. Rage, rage to live a little longer, to be among us now. Take the dares, the double-dares, and try. They work for some of us, may work for all of us.

Some people have cancer, are treated, and never again are troubled by the disease. They die of other causes, including old age. Others, like myself, less fortunate, must muster courage to start each day. Some days seem scarcely worth the effort, but on the chance that tomorrow, next week, the week after that, may yet be worthwhile, I double-dare myself to live.

Part of the fight for life is learning to live with the sharp-edged anxiety of not knowing how long we have to live. It is a horrendous predicament, because it seems to destroy any chance of planning ahead. For two years, I was obsessed with the need for a fixed date, a month, an approximate number of days. How else could I create priorities, choose my gravesite, make certain my affairs were in order, not waste a minute of life?

One day, nervous and sad, I talked to my lawyer about updating my will. It turned into a bigger job than I realized, for it meant designating everything I possess, working backwards into inventorying, and calling in an appraiser.

The whole effort was a slow task, consuming what little free time I had for several months. During those months, I began recovering from some radiation treatment, and my fear of imminent death began to subside. One day, I realized that I didn't have to keep working on the will because I wasn't dying, I was gradually recovering from the worst. What better time to dare myself to go on living? Thus, when I suddenly found that my next column would be my hundredth, I wrote:

"We share a sense of lost future, but we have gained the ability to do now the things we might have postponed indefinitely were it not for our death threat. Doing *now* takes guts and determination; I am constantly awed by the amount of courage that seriously ill Americans muster."

Courage can be visible, can be understood, can set an example for those who witness it. Let me share with you a letter from a reader who gave and bequeathed to her family the joy of living even when she knew she was dying.

Dear Jory:

I always liked your column, even before I was diagnosed with cancer. I liked your gutsyness, the will to survive. And when you asked cancer patients to write to you about their fears and other feelings, I thought, "I could tell her a few things." Hadn't I lost my brother at 50 to jaw cancer, and later my oldest sister to stomach cancer? The courage they both displayed never ceased to amaze me. . . .

I could identify with you when you told about walking and exercising to keep fit. I'd fought that battle myself, starting with rheumatoid arthritis 27 years ago, when my daughter Kathy was four years old. A year later, Bill was born, a beautiful son with platinum curls. My goal in life was to raise these two children, and though it was hard for me just to move, it was the happiest time of my life. . . .

My greatest physical enjoyment was bike riding. Though by spring of 1977, walking even one step was painful, I found I could ride my 24-inch bike for miles and enjoy the beautiful sights of nature. Usually my trip was the two miles to church for Mass. Sometimes I'd stop at the cleaner's or the bakery (the smell of their homemade bread and cookies was almost unbearably delicious). I never missed a day until the first week in December when I got caught in a snowstorm and came home looking like Frosty the Snowman, with snow on my hair and eyelashes. But it was wonderfully exhilarating.

. . . In May of 1978, I started having back trouble—the pain was like nothing I had known before. It would last about 18 hours and then go away. By June, it was round the clock and I went to the hospital. The doctor evidently didn't know too much about arthritis, because when he found I had been taking cortisone for years, he just took me off it cold turkey. He tried different drugs, but nothing helped (I developed an allergic reaction to one drug and almost died).

I came home after a month, without any diagnosis of my problem, unable to move from the neck down. My daughter

Kathy was upset and contacted an arthritis specialist who put me into another hospital for almost a month. When I came home I could walk with a walker, and finally a cane. Now I'm walking fairly well, considering.

But you know, Jory, I never felt like I was getting better. I couldn't sleep, couldn't eat, and suffered chronic anxiety. Sometime in October, I noticed lumps appearing on my arms, legs, breast, and stomach. I went to the doctor to have these checked. When he took a biopsy, he found it was lymph node cancer. Several doctors wanted me to take chemotherapy treatments but I refused because they said the outcome is unpredictable when one has been on steroid drugs. . . .

I feel pretty good some days; I could almost forget I don't have long to live. But other days, with my eyesight dimming from cataracts (from the cortisone), my skin paper-thin, and the bones in my hands and feet fused from arthritis, I wonder, why should I struggle to go on? Surely, God must have something better for me somewhere. . . .

Yet, I had the most beautiful birthday at my daughter's. And Christmas with her was like a gift: she kept a fire blazing, played Bing Crosby's Christmas album, and served the most delicious food. My three grandchildren were there. . . . If only I could see them get a little older. But then, my dear friend Father Bretz says, "God doesn't make mistakes, Dorine."

So, Jory, keep up the good work. Fight, fight, fight, and with God's help you will make it. I never thought I'd raise my Bill. But now he's almost 27 years old and he's still one of the lights of my life.

I think God has given me this extra time to prepare Kathy and Bill for my leaving them. We make the most of each day together, and we love one another. . . .

Remember the lines you quoted from Robert Frost. "The woods are lovely, soft and deep, But I have promises to keep, And miles to go before I sleep."

12.

In the Company of Others

"I can't bear the thought that I will simply
die and disappear. I need to know I
mattered."
All of us

Some of our most profound moments happen so simply. Norman
Hugo, the physician to whom I owe my life,[1] told me of one such
moment of his own, and it haunts me. His mother was dying of
cancer in his home. Norman came to the door of her room one
evening in time to hear one of his sons ask, "Grandma, are you
dying?"

"Yes, love, I am."

Norman said his son was sitting on the edge of her bed,
stroking her hair. He continued to stroke it as Norman, unnoticed, backed out of the door so that grandmother and grandson
could share whatever came next privately.

One evening long ago, I sat with my grandmother in her
hospital room. She had been hospitalized at least two weeks, but
each time I asked my parents what was wrong, their answers were
vague. Now my grandmother and I were alone together, watching
the sun drop behind some low buildings to the west. Suddenly my
grandmother said, "Darling, my sun is setting."

I was stunned. "No," I said. "No." She was silent. Her

husband had died two years earlier and I knew she ached with loneliness. But at that moment so did I. "Please don't leave me," I begged. She refused to argue it, even though tears rolled down her face and mine. Finally, she insisted I go home because it was late. She died alone sometime before morning. I was just seventeen and felt lost without her, this dearest person in my troubled adolescence.

A few years ago when I was moving and packing books, a faded card fell out of my grandmother's Bible. Written on it, in her elegant Spencerian script, was this:

> I wonder in what field today
> he chases butterflies at play,
> the little boy who ran away.[2]

It was as if my grandmother came alive. My living room, already flooded with midsummer sunlight, was filled with the sense of her presence. I knew with absolute certainty that she had written those lines as a grieving young mother trying to console herself for the tragic death of her eleven-year-old son. I had seen faded snapshots and sepia photographs of him—a solemn little fellow dressed in a Norfolk jacket and matching cap, whose knickers neatly met the tops of his high black hose. Now I saw him, this boy-uncle I never knew, not locked into solemnity by a camera lens, but laughing happily in an eternal game of chasing butterflies.

How long did my grandmother struggle with the pain of her loss before she found such imagery to soften the anguish of his death and begin letting go of it? I will never know, though at that moment her loving presence was so real I felt that if I asked her, she would answer. Unpredictable events and times of great emotional need evoke her memory for me in an overwhelming way. I sense her love, her warmth, her ability to comfort, and the poignant, stabbing awareness of my loss of her. Certain kinds of loss are never resolved entirely.

"I wonder in what field today . . ." The memorable triplet spun out into long threads of recollection, bringing me eventually to a story my grandmother would tell me after tucking me in for the night. It was about a little girl who followed three butterflies at dusk as they fluttered about looking for shelter among rows of tulips in a garden. The white butterfly sought a white tulip to snuggle down in; the yellow butterfly looked for a yellow tulip; the red butterfly found a red tulip. The little girl thought the butterflies would be even more comfortable in the pocket of her pinafore. She ran after them, caught them, and very gently put them into her pocket. Upstairs, undressing for bed, she carefully draped her pinafore over the back of a chair and whispered good night to the butterflies.

But in the morning they were gone. She looked for them everywhere (my grandmother would elaborate on all the places she searched, including the folds of the curtains, the last place left to look). Kneeling at the windowsill, the little girl put her head down and sobbed.

Finally, when her tears were exhausted, she stared mournfully out the window. And down below, in the garden, she saw the white butterfly poised on the white tulip, the yellow butterfly emerging from the yellow tulip, and the red butterfly lifting itself out of the red tulip. She pulled on her pinafore, and she ran down the stairs and out the door to join the butterflies in the sun-splashed garden.

That story was one of my grandmother's creations, and I am fairly sure she created it for me. In the time immediately following her death and my gradual letting go of my aching need for her, the story faded to a shadowy recollection of three butterflies, three tulips, and the security of being tucked into bed.

Sooner or later, every one of us must learn to let go, of dreams and hopes and people we love, and in the end, of life itself. Still, knowing the finality of death, even death that is welcome as an end to suffering, we hold onto life, reluctant to let go. Through sheer force of will, many of us live on despite a crushing amount of disease, in order to share a forthcoming rite of passage, a family marker: an anniversary, a graduation, a birthday, a marriage, the birth of a new grandchild, Thanksgiving, Christmas.

Yet I have seen too many instances where families are so panic-stricken by the prospect of death that the dying person somehow manages to extend his exhausted life simply because his family cannot let him go. This leads to the hospital situations we dread, the machines and tubes, and insane efforts to keep us breathing a few more days, another week or two. A desperate need born of guilt becomes crazed behavior when a family or a doctor demands that a patient be kept alive at all costs.

When such action is not in accord with our wishes, we usually have ourselves to blame. Had we been open with each other about our dying, had our families and our physicians clearly known that we do not want prolonged, mechanically sustained existence following brain death, then our right to refuse treatment would more likely be honored.[3]

Until the end of the eighteenth century, people managed their own dying. "[It] was a ritual organized by the dying person himself who presided over it and knew its protocol."[4] When a Jew felt his death was approaching, he sent for the Rabbi and to him would speak the *Vidui,* the confessional. He would ask God's forgiveness, reaffirm his faith in the one God, speak his last words, "Into Your hands do I now commit my soul," and turn his face to the wall. A Christian would lie on his back, facing heaven, lament his departure from the world, forgive those who needed forgiveness, reiterate his last will and testament, and request last rites.[5]

In a remarkable little paperback, *Western Attitudes Toward Death,* Philippe Ariès shows us how and why Western man lost not only his ability to accept death, but his ability to be in charge of the preparations for his death. From the eleventh to the eighteenth century: "death was a concern for the person threatened by it, and for him alone. Thus it was up to each person to express his ideas, his feelings, his wishes. For that he had available a tool: his last will and testament, which was more than simply a legal document for the disposal of property. From the thirteenth to the eighteenth century the will was the means by which each person could express—often in a very personal manner—his deep thoughts; his religious faith; his attachment to his possessions, to the beings he loved, and to God; and the decisions he had made to assure the salvation of his soul and the repose of his body."[6]

Death then was also public: people died surrounded by their entire families (children included), their friends and neighbors, the doctor (if one was present), and, of course, the cleric.

For a number of reasons, including industrialization and changing social ideas, Americans abandoned their right to manage their own deaths, and increasingly needed to deny the very fact of death. In the nineteenth century we came to believe that a dying individual should be protected from knowledge of his dying. In this century, we also protect ourselves from knowledge of another's dying by making certain it occurs in a hospital or nursing home, where, presumably,[7] others can deal with it much more effectively than we can.

Embalming the dead so that they will look as if they merely are resting is strictly an American practice. The wake is rapidly disappearing from industrialized Europe and "visitation," to use the odious term we Americans have let funeral directors impose on us, is anathema elsewhere. As Jessica Mitford said in *The American Way of Death,* "In England . . . the dead are not ordinarily embalmed, restored or viewed."[8]

The funeral industry has long been recognized as one of the biggest and most powerful money-making enterprises in the United States. Since 1885, when morticians began calling themselves "funeral directors," we have been increasingly willing to allow these profiteers to dictate to us the terms and the costs of visitation, the funeral, the burial. By letting everyone else decide where we will die and how our death will be organized, we do indeed allow ourselves to become cancer victims, trembling helplessly before approaching death rather than finding some measure of control and comfort in planning for it.

We need to reclaim our right to preside over our dying so that, as Edwin Shneidman says, "it fits [us]."[8] To this end, nonprofit memorial and funeral societies are active in forty-five states and across Canada, dedicated to simple burial or cremation, or first, if we wish, making an anatomical gift of our bodies for a year of cancer research. Hospice programs are growing partly in response to our deep wish to die at home. Autobiographies written by men and women who knew they were dying are readily available, so that we can learn from the experience of others the ways they prepared for their own deaths.

I answer letters from my readers that plead for help in quieting family opposition when they want to choose their gravesite or plan their own funeral. Yet I long for the kind of universal adult wisdom that knows planning for death does not hasten death. If our deepest wish is to plan, the wish should be honored: to know where our body or our ashes will be buried, under what tree or near what flowering shrub, can be wonderfully comforting.

I have made my own plans and found satisfaction in so doing. I have left binding legal instructions that give my physician the right to perform an autopsy, and deny any funeral director the right to embalm. My body is to be cremated; my ashes will be buried in a place of my choosing. I have written my own obituary and the brief wording for my headstone. I have named the memorial service I want and have chosen the music. I have done this so that no one will have to guess my wishes, and because making these simple decisions gives me a firm sense of directing parts of my own dying—for I may not have control over the rest.

We do not want to be taken away in an ambulance to die in a hospital. We have spent enough time in hospitals and want no more impersonal and regimented care. Earlier, we were stronger and could effectively protest. Now, we are too tired to fight strangers for our right to be in control of our lives to the very end.

My one reservation about the hospice movement is that, in trying to achieve uniform standards for hospice care, the planners may unwittingly try to program dying.

We do not want or need that. And we do not need some well-meaning stranger to "help us get in touch with our feelings," as one hospice nurse told me was her goal. We know what our feelings are. We want someone to understand them and let us talk about them a little.

Our dying cannot be converted into pseudoscientific stages

labeled "bargaining," or "denial." It is not comparable to a flu that follows a well-defined course. The notion of "stages of dying" gives many people a needed feeling of security—we are always more comfortable when we can paste labels on experiences that are mysteries. But a notion is not a fact.

I am filled with misgivings when I meet people who have read one book, attended one lecture, or taken one course on "death and dying" and believe they have become experts. I see how they muck up the lives of individuals who are indeed dying, by trying to direct those dying individuals into the "right" sequence. No one needs such presumptive and condescending "care." One has to read, listen, learn, think continuously, and be receptive to each new insight as it occurs.

Anyone who has gone beyond a superficial study of dying realizes that dying and its anguish are wholly individual. When we accept that idea we achieve a closeness with each other that lasts beyond death. The following letter came to me from the mother of an adolescent with whom I had been in touch:

Dear Jory Graham:

Tom died Friday, at peace with himself, his family, and God. He was at home, in my arms. When we left the hospital in July to begin "staying home," Tom was still in "good health," and would be seen by a doctor in our local cancer clinic.

Having Tom home again was so wonderful. His room was off the living room. That way he was part of all our activity. His brothers would stop in the first thing in the morning, say "Good day" or whatever, and be off to school. They would run back at lunchtime to eat beside him. After school, they returned again to read the evening newspaper or do homework by his bed, anything so he wouldn't feel left out.

After September, using his crutches became too painful, but Tom still got dressed every day he could to be up and around the house for a few hours.

He ate very little the last two months, but kept up his fluids quite well. He finally needed a wheelchair. We built a ramp and the boys pushed him everywhere.

We went shopping several times the week before he died.

He bought a rocket at the hobby shop, built and painted it, and shot it off. He bought an eight-track player for the family. He shopped through catalogs for his gifts for each of us. We would have gone out shopping again on Thursday, but the wind was 35 mph and he could not have breathed outdoors.

On Halloween, he sat with us and watched children in costume come to the door, and delighted in the ones I could coax in for a minute or two.

The weekend before he died, he sorted his things, and then he called in his brothers one by one, talked to them, told them he'd miss them but would always be there for them, and gave them his "gifts." He gave his tools to his dad. He gave his grandpa his deer antlers (he had brought in an eight-point buck last fall). He gave an uncle a favorite hat. And to all of us he gave his super-special moments to remember.

He and I were alone when he died. We prayed together, he in my arms, knowing we were asking God to take him home, and then he died. It was the saddest, yet most beautiful day of our lives.

I phoned my husband at work and the priest. The boys were gotten home. We prayed for strength and said our goodbys to Tom.

My father and my sister-in-law helped me wash Tom's hair. When she emptied the basin in the kitchen sink, bells began to play. The boys and my neighbor found the source, a musical snowman, wrapped in plastic, stored away behind several vases on the top shelf of the cupboard. The snowman had been there untouched for almost a year.

When Tom wanted our attention, he always rang a bell.

Once, a week or so before he died, I was sleeping on the couch when he rang it. (Sometimes it would be ten or fifteen minutes between bells, other times only four or five minutes. No, I didn't mind. I only feared I'd be too sound asleep to hear him when he needed me.) I rushed into his bedroom and asked sleepily, "What do you need, Tom?" His reply I will treasure forever: "Just a hug, Mom." Believe me, he got it. . . .

My friend Dr. Avery Danto Weisman has written about our right to have a "good death." Tom's was. Assisted, through his family's understanding, he gave his gifts. Enveloped in his mother's arms, enveloped in love and courage, he died warm and secure to the very end. And joined a mighty company of others who, preceding us, have shown how simple and quiet the moment of death can be. We need not fear that moment. Death is profound silence, nothing more.

I have one more letter to share with you.

Dear Jory:

I read your column with much admiration and interest. My husband died of cancer four months ago. He was 34 years old. We have four children, ages three to eleven. We all watched him deteriorate physically, but not mentally. When we found out he had cancer, we had two ways to go—waste our time being depressed, angry, and miserable, or live with that all-important something called *hope,* and make each day count.

At the end, my husband was unable to walk or even sit up, but he never lost his ability to smile and *hope.* He helped the kids with their homework from his bed—right to the end. Every day we tried to be creative, to make the day worthwhile and meaningful. The kids helped keep the charts for the shots I had to give him. I did striptease dances for him when I got ready for bed (designed to be provocative, but he found them humorous; oh, well). We read mysteries to him, and made him figure out "who-dun-it." We watched TV shows that we could discuss afterwards. We played games, with the kids helping him move his pieces. And we *hoped* and *laughed* and *loved*—much more rewarding than giving up and in to the disease.

I abhor the words of doctors, "There is no hope." Once you lose that precious commodity, you waste the time that means so much.

My husband died with dignity, and my children and I are able to grieve without guilt and regrets, for we shared not only his living but his dying in a positive way. . . . May God bless you.

I built a column around this letter. After it ran, someone wrote to ask how, in dying, anyone can have hope.

I answered saying that hope is not linked exclusively to a remote future but sometimes has its greatest meaning in a threatened present.

We hope we will have this day together and that the day will bring its own rewards. We hope that, despite our anguish over separation, we understand what we have meant, still mean, to one another: life companion to life companion, young husband to wife, parent to child, brother to sister, grandparent to grandchild, closest friend to closest friend. We hope that our living made a difference, that someone or something was changed because of us, perhaps made better or more memorable or more eloquent because of us.

We hope to join that company of others who were and will always be part of humanity. Dei gratia sum quod sum, *"By the grace of God I am what I am."*[10] *I was here, I made my home here. I leave my mark here.*

Appendix A

When Media Insensitivity Does Harm

From "A Time for Living," by Jory Graham

Every doctor who takes the Hippocratic Oath vows to "do no harm."

In this column, I ask my colleagues in the media to take a similar vow.

Specifically, I ask newscasters, newswriters, reporters, headline writers, and talk show hosts to quit labeling us cancer "victims," because it is so unfair, so belittling, so cruel.

No doctor describes his cancer patients as cancer "victims." Why should you? Is it because "victim" is such an easy handle, such a facile label? Most labels are detestable because they're loaded, as this one is. "Victim" says, "Here's someone we can/should/must pity."

How would you like to go through life as an object of pity?

Just listen to the way a talk show host introduces a guest who happens to have cancer: "With us today, cancer victim Michael Whoever." The TV host's words convey his sense of superiority —I'm well and powerful; here's someone you can feel sorry for, folks. Well, if Michael Whoever is a victim, he's solely a victim of the TV host's ignorance and assumption of the right to paste a derogatory label on his guest.

Michael Whoever is well enough to travel to a TV studio and well enough to be a guest on a show, but that doesn't count. That isn't enough to allow recognition of his separate identity. He's there because some producer wanted a cancer victim—"How did you feel when you learned you had cancer, Michael?" Never mind that Michael Whoever is nonplussed at being asked to reveal his deepest feelings on television. "Thank you for being our victim today, Michael."

Victim is a noun. When it becomes the only noun attached to one's name, it supersedes personhood and achievement. It reduces the "victim" to a one-dimensional stereotype, whereas everybody else is still three-dimensional.

The condescension, the insult in the label "victim" is that the word insinuates passivity. Something is done to someone who is both helpless to prevent it and helpless in the face of it—like the person who is in the middle of a three-car crash, or the one who becomes the target of a sniper's bullet. But most cancer patients are not helpless. They fight back.

They survive the first terrible round and they get back on their feet, back to their work, back to their positions in their families, back to affirming life. How can they possibly be victims when they're fighting back?

The cumulative impact of the press and broadcast media is enormous. Eventually the combined insistence that people who have cancer are "victims" will become too overwhelming to counter. Even now the cancer "victims" I see exploited on TV are too intimidated to protest the label. It just makes me weep.

So long as those who have cancer are viewed as pitiable and helpless, no one will ever open better job opportunities for them, or bank loans, or insurance possibilities, or long-term mortgages. And on a social level they'll be avoided because virtually nobody knows how to be comfortable in the presence of victims. The implications of their helplessness simply create guilt and unease.

We who are in the press and broadcasting like to think of ourselves as champions of liberty, righters of wrongs. It's time to understand the wrongness of labeling everyone who has cancer a "victim." You wouldn't want it for yourself or your mate or your child or your parent. In fairness, then, quit slapping the label on us.

Appendix B

ONE/FOURTH
THE ALLIANCE FOR CANCER PATIENTS
AND THEIR FAMILIES

STATEMENT OF PURPOSE

One/Fourth's goals, and the deep conviction of its founders and members, are expressed in its Statement of Purpose:

To foster understanding of the physical, emotional, social and financial needs of cancer patients.

To work for the rights of all who live with cancer, including:
The right of each patient to know his diagnosis;
The right of each patient to know his treatment options;
The right of each patient to skillful and unstinting pain relief;
The right to totally modern medical care;
The right to affordable medical treatment;
The right to full acceptance in the job market;
The right to full acceptance in society.

Appendix C

Why "I give you nine months" is nonsense

From "A Time for Living," by Jory Graham

One gets a diagnosis of cancer and is stunned. One's first reaction is, "I'm going to die," yet the first question is, "How long have I got to live?"

"Beware the physician who responds with a specific answer, 'I give you nine months,'" warns Dr. John Merrill, of Northwestern University Medical School. "That doctor doesn't know as much about cancer as you want your doctor to know. You should immediately say that you want a second opinion from a cancer specialist (an oncologist).

"The oncologist's answer won't be more reassuring, but it will be more honest: 'I don't know how much time you have left.'"

I have yet to meet an oncologist who will predict life span, but I have now heard from several hundreds of people who were told by their own doctor or a surgeon to whom they were referred for confirmation of a diagnosis that they (or a member of their family who has cancer) have only X months to live. "Yet," says Dr. Merrill, "such a prediction is not possible, for cancer is inherently unpredictable. Often patients with advanced cases of the disease will recover and live years without further problems; often, patients with very early, nonvirulent, eminently treatable cancers will go downhill so rapidly as to shock every physician concerned with them."

Who, then, is the physician who announces, "I give you X months"—as if he has that to give? How can any doctor assume a direct line to God? Furthermore, if the doctor is able to give you X months, why not be generous and give X years?

A minority of doctors have a sense of omnipotence which is really sheer arrogance. Their attitude is, "I know from as much as I know that you have X months to live." But the majority of physicians who make such a prediction have your best interests at heart. They want to answer your questions honestly. They know how much anxiety you feel because they cannot give you an accurate prediction, and so they blunder. They predict a time span that is inherently unpredictable.

All of us believe that if we only could know how much time we have left we would plan accordingly. For months, I yearned for an actual deadline because not having one was so intolerable. But a faulty prediction of life span is even more intolerable. Imagine expecting you will die by a certain date. The date arrives, yet you are quite alive. Ironically, that's not always joyful. Dr. Elisabeth Kübler-Ross has shown us that someone in this position is "not able to live and enjoy himself and is not able to die; is angry, and everybody around him upsets him because they are kind of standing around waiting for his death to occur and death does not occur."

Resigning yourself to die at an arbitrarily selected time isn't fair to you or your family or friends. All you do is create the bleakest depression. Whatever amount of time is left to each of us should not be destroyed by another person, no matter how well-meaning he is.

Yes, you want to know because you want to put your affairs in order, decide whether to quit a job you hate, give up what might be a futile attempt to get a higher degree, or plan to have another child. But a prediction of your life span isn't the answer because there's no way it can be accurate. Cancer, like life itself, asks us to accept uncertainty.

Patients Push M.D.s to Predict the Unpredictable: Life Span

From "A Time for Living," by Jory Graham

No doctor wants to give a diagnosis of cancer. All doctors know that such a diagnosis will be viewed as a death sentence. Why, then, do so many of them insist on sealing the verdict with an "I give you six months"?

With cancer, predictions of life span cannot be accurate. . . . Here is Dr. John Merrill of the Northwestern University Medical School, a medical oncologist at its cancer center:

"I want to emphasize that it is not that I won't predict but that I *cannot* predict. A discussion of average life span of groups of patients is, of course, possible, but of no help. Let's say that for a specific tumor, statistics show that eighty percent of patients with this tumor will be alive at the end of one year, and twenty percent will be dead. But there's no way of knowing which group an individual patient will be in. That's why I cannot predict. This is the key issue, but it's precisely where a breach of faith occurs.

"A patient may assume, 'Gee, this is a basic question; if this man can't answer it he doesn't know as much about cancer as my referring physician thinks he does.' Or, 'If he won't answer this question for me he's not being as honest as I insist my doctors be. He was honest in telling me the diagnosis, honest in telling me where the cancer has spread and forthright in suggesting his treatment. He outlined the potential benefits and the side effects. But he seems not to want to level with me on this matter of how long I am going to live.'

"That patient will then say to me that he is going to find

someone who will lay it on the line for him—and he will. He will find a physician who can be coerced into giving him a day, or a number of weeks, or a number of months. I have seen patients so desperate for a time frame they go from doctor to doctor, looking for the best offer, so to speak. I have had patients say, 'Dr. L. gave me two good years, Dr. R. gave me one. I am therefore going to Dr. L. because he's twice as good.'

"It is frustrating to lose a patient's confidence because of my inability to predict life span, yet all I can say is, I regret it. The frustration over being so ignorant is not very easily described. I wish I knew, I *wish* I knew more about it, but I don't, so I try to work with what I do know."

Later, in the same interview, Dr. Merrill said, "Our lack of knowledge in some areas of the practice of cancer medicine is substantial. The only relief is in knowing that some of these areas are opening up to our limited skills and that in a few more years we will be much more knowledgeable. Five years from now, I will look back and think how primitive we were, how primitive were our methods for handling certain kinds of tumors.

"Even now I look back at what we were doing in 1972 and can't believe the ignorance with which we dealt with some malignancies. Once, if you didn't cure cancer with radical surgery, everything else was catch-up. Now, several types of cancer are curable with radiation therapy or chemotherapy or a combination of both. We are gaining knowledge and some cancer controls. Still, I don't think we'll ever be able to predict life span; cancer doesn't lend itself to that."

Appendix D

Some Medical Opinions on Radiation Therapy as Primary Treatment for Early Breast Cancer

I have no idea how many physicians read my 1978 columns informing readers that mastectomy was no longer the only acceptable form of primary treatment for early breast cancer. However, dozens of physicians wrote to me; here are excerpts from a few of their letters:

> I am delighted that finally the word of conservative treatment is getting to women who undergo biopsies for breast cancer. We began treating carefully selected patients with early tumors with irradiation as long as twenty years ago, but we have still not made much headway in distributing this knowledge and information to patients. My very best wishes for your continued efforts in every woman's behalf. . . .
>
> Eleanor D. Montague, M.D.
> Professor of Radiotherapy
> M. D. Anderson Hospital and Tumor Institute
> University of Texas System Cancer Center

You are without a question a beacon in this very difficult and trying area. . . . I agree with you . . . it is the physician's responsibility to convey to patients the alternatives in terms of management of a primary breast malignancy. Our own experience illustrates that when one matches the surgical results versus the radiation therapy results, they are equally viable alternatives. In our experience with more than 150 cases now, we are able to demonstrate 92 percent five-year survival rate without recurrent disease. There is no surgical series I know of that is doing as well. My congratulations on a beautifully conceived and wonderfully written group of columns on primary management for cancer of the breast using radiation therapy. We need spokeswomen like yourself. . . .

Luther W. Brady, M.D.
Professor and Chairman
Department of Radiation Therapy and Nuclear Medicine
Hahnemann Medical College Hospital of Philadelphia

I would only interject one cautionary note: radiation therapy without mastectomy is not suitable for all women with early stage breast cancer. Women with heavy, pendulous breasts are more difficult to treat technically and do not get as satisfactory a cosmetic result. Also, women with large tumors, relative to the size of the breast (a tumor 5 centimeters or more) probably need to have the breast removed in order to remove the tumor. . . . I am quite pleased to see accurate articles in the lay press on this subject since I am afraid the medical profession is moving much too slowly in this respect. . . .

Leonard R. Prosnitz, M.D.
Professor of Therapeutic Radiology
Department of Therapeutic Radiology
Yale University School of Medicine

The columns that you have written are the kind I feel are necessary to bring home to women with breast lumps that there are viable alternatives to mastectomy. Your columns were . . . to the point and directed to the patient. It is my feeling that it will be the patient who will bring about these important changes, rather than the surgeon. . . . Continue the good work. . . .

Carl M. Mansfield, M.D.
Professor and Chairman
Department of Radiation Therapy
University of Kansas Medical Center

I appreciate your expert and precise reporting. . . . I've enclosed one of my articles on the subject of limited breast surgery. The title is a bit misleading; if I were to do it over again, I would not call it 'segmental mastectomy' since most of the operative procedures done in the United States are really large biopsies rather than segmental operations. . . .

Rodney R. Million, M.D.
Professor
Division of Radiation Therapy
University of Florida College of Medicine

Lastly, a radiation oncologist at a major university hospital wrote:

We do not treat early breast cancer with excision of tumor and radiation therapy at this medical center because our department of surgery won't hear of it. If my wife had breast cancer, she would not be treated here.

Appendix E

Organizations mentioned in the text may be contacted at the following locations:

National Cancer Institute
National Institutes of Health
Bethesda, Maryland 20205

American Cancer Society
777 Third Avenue
New York, New York 10017

One/Fourth, The Alliance For Cancer Patients And Their Families
36 South Wabash Avenue
Chicago, Illinois 60603

Make Today Count, Inc.
National Headquarters
514 Tampa Building, Box 303
Burlington, Iowa 52601

National Committee on the Treatment of Intractable Pain
9300 River Road
Potomac, Maryland 20854

Notes

Chapter 1

1. This figure excludes non-melanoma skin cancers estimated to be about 400,000) and carcinomas *in situ* (for which there is no estimate available). These cancer incidence rates are based upon data from the National Cancer Institute's SEER Program (1973–1977).
2. "A Time for Living"; in Chicago, "A Time to Live."

Chapter 2

1. Jean Anouilh, *The Lark,* adapted by Lillian Hellman (New York: Random House, 1956), pp. 75–76.

Chapter 3

1. Hans O. Mauksch, Ph.D., "The Organizational Context of Dying," in *Death: The Final Stage of Growth,* ed. Elisabeth Kübler-Ross, M.D. (Englewood Cliffs, N.J.: Prentice-Hall, 1975), p. 17.
2. Nuclear medicine now has much newer, faster equipment than this, though it may not yet be in general use.
3. See Appendix A, "When Media Insensitivity Does Harm."
4. One/Fourth addresses the social and human aspects of cancer on a broad scale, complementing the American Cancer Society's work on medical advances against the disease. (See Appendix B for One/Fourth's statement of purpose.)
5. Leonard R. Derogatis, Ph.D., Martin Abeloff, M.D., and Nick Melisaratos, M.H.S., "Psychological Coping Mechanisms and Survi-

val Time in Metastatic Breast Cancer," *Journal of the American Medical Association*, 5 October 1979, p. 1504.

6. Dylan Thomas, "Do not go gentle into that good night," from *The Collected Poems of Dylan Thomas* (New York: New Directions, 1946), p. 128.

Chapter 4

1. Policy at most hospitals binds nurses from revealing a diagnosis to a patient. Hence, nurses are forced to be evasive and to lie. But nurses are no better at lies or evasions than families, so, in the end, it is almost always nurses who inadvertently give the lie away. They are not to be blamed so much as pitied, for they genuinely deplore the dishonesty. On the other hand, their nursing associations could take a strong position on this issue, but most have not.

2. As Susan Sontag observed in her book *Illness as Metaphor* (New York: Farrar, Straus & Giroux, 1977), on page 7: "As long as a particular disease is treated (perceived) as an evil, invincible predator, not just a disease, most people will indeed be demoralized by learning what disease they have."

3. William Whitney, "Eternal Father, Strong to Save" (1860).

4. *Chicago Tribune*, 15 August 1977.

5. August M. Kaspar, M.D., "The Doctor and Death," in *The Meaning of Death*, ed. Herman Feifel (New York: McGraw-Hill, 1959), pp. 259–70. This same observation appears in virtually all studies on death and dying.

6. Professor of Bioethics, Georgetown University, Washington, D.C.

7. Robert M. Veatch, "When Should the Patient Know?", *Barrister* 8, no. 1 (Winter 1981): 17.

8. Example: The old joke about the five-year-old who is dragging a little suitcase endlessly around the block he lives on. A neighbor stops the child and asks kindly, "What are you doing?" The child says, "I'm running away." The neighbor chuckles and asks, "Oh, then why do you keep running around this same block?" The child says, "I'm not allowed to cross the street."

9. Elisabeth Kübler-Ross, M.D., *On Death and Dying* (New York: Macmillan, 1969), pp. 38–49.

10. See discussion of "stages" in Edwin Shneidman, *Voices of Death* (New York: Harper & Row, 1980), pp. 110–11.

11. Nathan Schnaper, M.D., "Psychosocial Aspects of Management of the Patient with Cancer," *Medical Clinics of North America* 60, no. 5 (September 1977): 1153–54.

12. A paraphrase of a statement made by oncologist Lucien Israël, M.D., head of the Hôpital Franco-Musulman, Bobigny, France, on the *Dick*

Cavett Show at the time Dr. Israël's book *Conquering Cancer* (Random House, 1978) appeared in American translation. When asked about a patient's right to know his diagnosis of cancer, Dr. Israël exploded, "Outrageous to have the secret to a man's life and not reveal it." The statement is all the more remarkable since in France less than ten percent of all cancer patients are ever told their diagnosis.

13. "Psychosocial Aspects of Management of the Patient with Cancer," p. 1153.

14. See especially "When Should the Patient Know?" pp. 6–20. See also these legal cases: Natanson v. Kline, 186 Kan. 393, 350 P.2d 1093 (1960); Schloendorff v. New York Hospital, 211 N.Y. 127, 129; 105 N.E. 92, 93 (1914), in which Justice Cardozo, then a New York State Court of Appeals judge, enunciated the principle of self-determination, that "every human being of adult years and sound mind has a right to determine what shall be done with his own body."

Chapter 5

1. Five-year survival figures are simply medical parameters, not guarantees of cure. They came into use at the turn of the century, when surgery became a treatment for cancer and a yardstick was needed by which to judge accomplishment. Five-year survival rates have improved since those early days:

1900–1920s	approximately 1 in 10 survived
1930s	less than 1 in 5 survived
1950s	1 in 4 survived
1970s	1 in 3 survived

The National Cancer Institute's End Results Report No. 5 stated in 1979 that forty-one percent of all patients with cancer can be expected to survive five years without evidence of disease, an improvement over the early 1970s.

2. Actor John Wayne was one example. In 1964, John Wayne's left lung and part of his right lung were removed because of lung cancer. To encourage other cancer patients he declared: "I licked the Big C." And so he had, until January of 1979, when his stomach was removed because of a different cancer (tests also revealed cancer in his gastric lymph nodes). Some unfortunate people have had three or even four primary cancers. John Wayne died at age seventy-two, on June 11, 1979.

3. For example, in 1971, forty percent of all patients with Wilm's Tumor could expect to live for five years. But only eight years later (1979), the number of patients surviving Wilm's Tumor for more than five years had leaped to ninety percent.

Other remarkable gains:

	Approximate percentage surviving five years	
	Pre-1972	1979
Rhabdomyosarcoma and Ewing's sarcoma	10 to 20	60 to 70
Adult Acute Leukemia	no long-term survivors	12.5 (4 years)
Small cell lung cancer	no long-term survivors (weeks to a few months)	10 (median survival one year)
Hodgkin's disease		
Stage I	20	90 to 95
Stage IIA	less than 20	90

4. See the two columns in Appendix C. Both are based on interviews with John M. Merrill, M.D., and clearly illustrate the inherent unpredictability of life span when cancer is the disease.

Chapter 6

1. The term *surgery* refers to a discipline of knowledge, skill, and research, of which surgical procedures (operations) are frequently a part. But, since all of us in the laity use the word *surgery* as a synonym for *surgical procedure*, this book follows lay usage.
2. William T. Moss, M.D., William N. Brand, M.D., and Hector Battifora, M.D., *Radiation Oncology: Rationale, Technique, Results*, 5th ed. (St. Louis: C.V. Mosby Co., 1979); Gilbert H. Fletcher, M.D., *Textbook of Radiotherapy*, 3rd ed. (Philadelphia: Lea & Febiger, 1980).
3. Single cancer cells or little clusters of cancer cells which, by the time of surgery at one site, have made their way through the bloodstream to other locations.
4. Umberto Veronesi, M.D., et al., "Comparing Radical Mastectomy with Quadrantectomy, Axillary Dissection, and Radiotherapy in Patients with Small Cancers of the Breast," *New England Journal of Medicine,* 2 July 1981, pp. 6–11.
5. Radical surgery is so universal that at least two physicians have gone a step further and are now actually removing breasts from women *before* the breast(s) show any symptoms of cancer—a measure that relies on encouragement of fear. This was reported under the heading "Radical Prevention" in *Time* magazine on July 9, 1979: "Preventive surgery for breast cancer even before the disease is

diagnosed? The idea sounds highly unpromising, but at least two surgeons are now performing such prophylactic mastectomies. Dr. Henry P. Leis Jr. of New York City limits the surgery to women who have already had one cancerous breast removed. In 17% of these patients, reports *Medical World News*, tissue examinations revealed undiagnosed cancer in the [other] breast. Dr. Charles S. Rogers of Bay City, Mich., has taken the theory a step further by performing double mastectomies on women who had no apparent signs of the disease but were judged prone to cancer because of family history, breast tissue characteristics and other clues. The key question: Are women who take this drastic step better off than others who simply wait and see?" Somehow, this seems like the equivalent of decapitation to prevent meningitis.

6. MEDICAL BREAKTHROUGHS OFTEN GO UNNOTICED BY DOCTORS, A STUDY SUGGESTS, reported a front-page *Wall Street Journal* column item on June 26, 1979. "That conclusion comes from two University of Michigan researchers, Drs. Jeoffrey Stross and William Harlan, who surveyed 228 doctors attending continuing-education seminars at the university. The doctors were asked how they would treat two imaginary diabetes patients afflicted with a type of blindness common to diabetics. Most proved ignorant of a treatment for the blindness hailed 18 months ago as an important medical advance.

"Although the treatment had been discussed in various medical journals, only 33% of the doctors said they would use it in the hypothetical cases. Only 28% of the family physicians and 46% of the internists were familiar with study results, released in 1976, on the treatment.

"*Of those familiar with the treatment, only a fourth had learned of it from medical journals. Most heard about it from a colleague, the study says.*"

7. After my first mastectomy, I was commissioned to write a four-part newspaper series, "Comeback from Breast Cancer," for the Field Newspaper Syndicate (August, 1976). In the series I was candid about women's feelings vis-à-vis mutilative surgery. I wrote about our anger at what was done to us, and about the long period of mourning that follows loss of a loved part of ourselves; I told about the excruciating worry over sexual acceptance, and about our deep sense of despair. I said that, around the third day, "a woman's surgeon insists she stop crying. Because she's dependent on him, she does—just long enough for him to get in and out of her room." Mastectomees wrote to me for more than two years after the series ran. Apparently, it was the first time anything had appeared in their newspapers that so clearly verbalized their deepest feelings. I was

and am grateful to women whose names I do not know but whose mastectomies were performed by the same surgeon who performed mine; these women read "Comeback from Breast Cancer" and finally admitted their real feelings to him. And he had the grace to tell me.

8. Cornelius Ryan and Kathryn Morgan Ryan, *A Private Battle* (New York: Simon & Schuster, 1979), p. 85. The impotence-incontinence figures the urologist cited were inaccurate. The actual frequencies of impotence and incontinence "are nearly 100% and 5%, respectively, following radical prostatectomy but for radiation treatments these figures are approximately 30% to 40% and 0% to 2% respectively," according to the *Journal of the American Medical Association*, 18 May 1979, pp. 1912–15.

9. *A Private Battle*, pp. 87–88. Cornelius Ryan never saw this urologist again. He spent the next three months researching prostate cancer, determined to find a less offensive alternative. Eventually, he opted for radiation and was so treated.

10. The bibliography is now incorporated in "An Alternative to Mastectomy." See note 12 below.

11. Cancer of the pancreas and some colorectal cancers are notable exceptions, eluding early diagnosis and undiscoverable until they have metastasized.

12. These columns, two wrap-up columns, and the aforementioned bibliography have been updated and printed in a thirty-two-page booklet, "An Alternative to Mastectomy," available through Andrews and McMeel, 4400 Johnson Drive, Fairway, Kansas 66205.

13. See Appendix D, "Some Medical Opinions on Radiation Therapy as Primary Treatment for Early Breast Cancer."

14. Dr. Umberto Veronesi and his colleagues (see note 4 above) concluded that "patients with early breast cancer who are treated with quadrantectomy and axillary dissection plus radiotherapy have the same survival rate and the same incidence of local and distant recurrences as patients who are treated with the Halsted mastectomy. On the basis of this study, radical mastectomy appears to involve unnecessary mutilation in patients with carcinoma of the breast measuring less than 2 cm and without palpable axillary nodes." "Comparing Radical Mastectomy," p. 11.

15. Dr. Jerome Urban and a few other surgeons out-radical radical mastectomies by also surgically exploring a woman's mediastinum (the median partition of the chest cavity) and neck in extensive thoracervical dissections; what Dr. E. F. Lewison calls "surgery bordering on 'humanectomy . . . limited solely by the ability of the human remnant to survive.'" Edward Frederick Lewison, M.D., *Breast Cancer and Its Diagnosis and Treatment* (Baltimore: Williams & Wilkins Co., 1955), p. 218.

16. Walter G. Gunn, M.D., J.D., "The Law of Medical Malpractice: Its Contact Points with Radiation Therapy," in *Radiotherapy in Malignant Diseases*, ed. Carl M. Mansfield, M.D., F.A.C.R. (Garden City, N.Y.: Medical Examination Publishing Company, to be published in 1982.)

17. One should also remember that the physician-patient relationship is a contract.

18. Barbara J. McNeil, M.D., Ph.D., Ralph Weichselbaum, M.D., and Stephen G. Pauker, M.D., "Fallacy of the Five-Year Survival in Lung Cancer," *New England Journal of Medicine*, 21 December 1978, pp. 1397–1401.

19. From the authors' response to comments on "Fallacy of the Five-Year Survival," *New England Journal of Medicine*, 19 April 1979, p. 928.

20. "Fallacy of the Five-Year Survival," p. 1397.

21. Keith I. Marton, M.D., to the editor, *New England Journal of Medicine*, 19 April 1979, p. 928.

22. Ibid., Jacobo Wortsman, M.D., F.A.C.P., to the editor.

23. University of Rochester School of Medicine and Dentistry, *Clinical Oncology for Medical Students and Physicians*, 5th ed. (Rochester, N.Y.: American Cancer Society, 1978), p. 75.

Chapter 7

1. Avery D. Weisman, M.D., *Coping with Cancer* (New York: McGraw-Hill, 1979), p. 18.

2. As diagnostic testing becomes more exotic (and more expensive), it also becomes more dangerous, as with arteriograms. Hence, full disclosure is now mandated for diagnostic procedures, too.

3. As patients, we need to learn that it's all right to shout, "I hate having cancer," but this almost assumes that doctors, nurses, families, concerned friends understand our need to rage and will tolerate at least some of the outbursts when they occur.

4. Hormonal ablation therapy. By eliminating the hormonal output of the ovaries, metastases can be vastly slowed for certain women who have not reached menopause. Life is extended, often by several years, for some sixty percent of all women who receive hormonal ablation therapy for breast cancer.

5. I was getting daily radiation at the time and was both ill and exhausted from it. I felt too weak to contend with major surgery as well, whereas more radiation to another site would merely increase the side effects I already knew I could tolerate. The problem with radiation therapy was its slowness (approximately fifteen weeks to destroy all ovarian function); a surgeon could remove both ovaries in some thirty-five minutes and that would be that.

6. A senior medical student, volunteering some free time to help answer some of my reader mail, was wonderfully competent in answering medical questions but inept at providing that elusive quality, hope. He would write to a reader, "You must maintain hope," a phrase he learned from the attending physicians he followed as they made rounds. One day I asked him, "How do you expect this reader to get hope? How is it packaged? Where can he buy it? 'You must have hope' is meaningless unless you find some quality in his life revealed in his letter that you can expand for him. It might be that patient's courage in discussing a frightening problem. Build on his courage. That is one way you, as a doctor, create hope."

7. Sir Sidney Smith, C.B.E., L.L.D., M.D., F.R.C.P., *Mostly Murder* (New York: McKay, 1959), p. 27.

8. The number (800-638-6694) is the toll-free listing for the Cancer Information Service, a twenty-four-hour hotline recognized by the National Cancer Institute. Its staff answers any questions about cancer, drawing on information from comprehensive cancer centers across the United States, N.C.I., state and local health departments, and the American Cancer Society.

9. Unfortunately, compassion and good listening often disappear under swollen patient loads. For example: A town of 120,000 people is likely to have only three oncologists. Suppose the town supports four community and private hospitals. If each doctor is responsible daily for sixty cancer patients distributed among the four hospitals, and if each doctor works a minimum of twelve hours daily, he has a total of eight hours each day for patients—a maximum of eight minutes per patient.

Chapter 8

1. Jerome H. Jaffe, M.D., and William R. Martin, M.D., "Narcotic Analgesics and Antagonists," chap. 15 in *Basis of Therapeutics*, 5th ed., ed. Louis S. Goodman and Alfred Gilman (New York: Macmillan, 1975), p. 261.

2. David S. Shimm, M.D., Gerald L. Logue, M.D., Allan A. Maltbie, M.D., and Sally Dugan, R.N., "Medical Management of Chronic Cancer Pain," *Journal of the American Medical Association*, 1 June 1979, p. 2408.

3. William T. Beaver, M.D., "Management of Cancer Pain with Parenteral Medication," *Journal of the American Medical Association*, 12 December 1980, p. 2653.

4. See the following studies: Richard R. Marks, M.D., and Edward J. Sachar, M.D., "Undertreatment of Medical Inpatients with Narcotic Analgesics," *Annals of Internal Medicine* 78, no. 20 (February 1973):

173–81; "Narcotic Analgesics and Antagonists" (note 1 above); "Medical Management of Chronic Cancer Pain" (note 2 above); "Management of Cancer Pain with Parenteral Medication" (note 3 above).

5. Raymond W. Houde, M.D., chief and attending physician of the Memorial Hospital for Cancer and Allied Diseases and head of the Laboratory of Analgesic Studies at the Sloan-Kettering Institute for Cancer Research.

6. Such belief comes only after a family has witnessed the pain-free death of one of its members. Even then the family is incredulous, and often somebody in the family writes to me saying, "You were right, but I didn't believe you until it happened with the death of our father."

7. Robert G. Twycross, M.A., D.M., M.R.C.P., Consulting Physician, Sir Michael Sobell House (a hospice), the Churchill Hospital, Oxford, England. Dr. Twycross has published over twenty-five articles on pain treatment and has contributed nine chapters to as many medical textbooks.

8. Robert G. Twycross, M.A., D.M., M.R.C.P., "Disease of the Central Nervous System: Relief of Terminal Pain," *British Medical Journal*, 25 October 1975, p. 212.

9. Kathleen M. Foley, M.D., "The Management of Pain of Malignant Origin," chap. 18 in *Current Neurology*, vol. 2, ed. H. R. Tyler and D. M. Dawson (Boston: Houghton-Mifflin, 1979), p. 279.

10. Jules Michelet, *Satanism and Witchcraft: A Study in Medieval Superstition* (New York: Citadel Press, 1939), pp. 77–78.

11. John Huizinga, *The Waning of the Middle Ages* (Garden City: Doubleday Anchor Books, 1954), p. 11.

12. Michel Foucault, *Discipline and Punish: The Birth of the Prison*, tr. Alan Sheridan (New York: Pantheon Books, 1978), pp. 33, 34.

13. Ibid.

14. Ibid., p. 46.

15. John Calvin, *On God and Political Duty*, ed. John T. McNeill (Indianapolis: Bobbs-Merrill, 1956), pp. 69, 89.

16. William James, *The Varieties of Religious Experience* (New York: Mentor Books, 1960), p. 87.

17. Gerald L. Klerman, M.D., "Psychotropic Hedonism *vs.* Pharmacological Calvinism," *The Hastings Center Report* (Institute of Society, Ethics and the Life Sciences, New York) 2, no. 4 (September 1972): 1–3. Dr. Klerman is Professor of Psychiatry at Harvard Medical School.

18. Howard Haggard, M.D., *Devils, Drugs and Doctors* (New York: Blue Ribbon Books, 1929), p. 108.

19. From *Thanatos*, the Greek god of death.
20. Exclusive of euthanasia societies, which have been with us since the last century.
21. William Lamer, Jr., M.D., Medical Director, Hospice of Marin (Marin County, California), to Sandol Stoddard, *The Hospice Movement* (New York: Vintage Books, 1978), pp. 67–68.
22. New York: McGraw-Hill, 1978.
23. People who have severe, chronic arthritis know this pain well, and they may well wish they *could* die, just to escape agony, but they are spared the cancer patient's knowledge of pain as a signal of impending death. By and large, we are disgracefully unsympathetic to their plight. Our attitude is that, since those who have arthritis won't die of it, they ought through sheer will power to be able to master their pain and stop complaining.
24. Edward D. Viner, M.D., and D. Jeffery Hurtzel, M.D., "The Hospice Movement in the United States," in *Over Fifty-Five*, ed. Theodore Duncan, M.D., a Pennsylvania Hospital textbook to be published in 1982.
25. Ibid.
26. Arkansas, California, Idaho, Kansas, Nevada, New Mexico, North Carolina, Oregon, Texas, and Washington.
27. From a current brochure describing the National Committee on the Treatment of Intractable Pain.

Chapter 9
1. Cancer, an inherently unpredictable disease, defies accurate prediction of life span to the degree that no reputable oncologist will give one, especially at the time of diagnosis, which is when all patients beg for it. See Appendix C.
2. A cure-all idea floating about for more than one hundred years, now coupled with "colonic irrigation" and odd diets that forbid coffee as a beverage.
3. Other unhelpful platitudes in the same category include: "I could be dead tomorrow, run over by a car"; "We don't understand God's plan for people. We have to accept it"; "You have to do what your doctors say, because they know best"; "I knew somebody younger than you who had it worse than you"; "This is something that can happen to any of us"; and, to the patient who has just come through mutilative surgery, "Be thankful you're alive."
4. November 30, 1977.
5. From the transcript.

Chapter 10
1. "Comeback from Breast Cancer," Field Newspaper Syndicate, 1976.
2. The surgeon who took off my breasts was offended by the expression

of naked feelings in my "Comeback from Breast Cancer" articles, and said so. He had been performing mastectomies for more than thirty years; not one other patient ever told him she felt destroyed. I said, "You don't allow confessions of hurt. You tell us we must think positively and 'get on with the business of living.'" Months later, he gained stature in my eyes by telling me that a number of his patients had discussed my articles with him and that he was beginning to understand the bottomlessness of their wounds. (See chapter 6, note 7.)

3. Melvin V. Gerbie, M.D., "Malignant Neoplasms of the Vulva," in *Gynecology and Obstetrics*, vol. 1, ed. John J. Sciarra, M.D. (Hagerstown, Md.: Harper & Row, 1977), p. 4.

4. Ibid., pp. 2–3.

5. Alex Comfort, M.B., Ph.D., D.Sc., ed., *Sexual Consequences of Disability* (Philadelphia: George F. Stickley, 1978).

6. Lilian Lieber, Ph.D., Marjorie M. Plumb, Ph.D., Martin Gerstenzang, M.D., and Jimmie Holland, M.D., "The Communication of Affection Between Cancer Patients and Their Spouses," in *Psychosomatic Medicine* 38, no. 6 (November–December, 1976): 379–89.

7. Thomas O. Mooney, Theodore M. Cole, M.D., and Richard A. Chilgren, M.D., *Sexual Options for Paraplegics and Quadriplegics* (Boston: Little, Brown, 1975).

8. Joan Kron, "Designing a Better Place to Die," *New York*, 7 March 1976, p. 48.

9. Ibid.

10. Note that in the gynecologist's text quoted above (see note 3), the author says, "Counseling before and support after treatment are important," but he neglects to offer counseling insights to clinicians. It is my belief that, whenever a textbook describes a mutilative surgical procedure, the author is obligated to offer his colleagues insights into healing emotional wounds left by the surgery.

11. Or the vagina, the tongue, part of the face or head, a leg, an arm, the penis.

12. Neither are doctors trained to understand that a patient's depression following mutilative surgery conceals unexpressed rage over what the patient perceives as a permanently compromised life. Even if physicians recognized the degree of their patients' silent fury and self-loathing, how many would feel comfortable with, or give the necessary time to, helping create a resolution? How many physicians will even take the time to find and refer these patients to a qualified medical colleague, a psychiatrist or a psychoanalyst, who understands problems of human sexuality and cancer?

13. Harry S. Goldsmith, M.D., and Edgardo S. Alday, M.D., "Role of the Surgeon in the Rehabilitation of the Breast Cancer Patient,"

Cancer 28 (December, 1971), American Cancer Society: 1672–75.

14. Memorial Hospital is the treatment facility of Memorial Sloan-Kettering Cancer Center, New York City.

15. A surgical procedure for cancer of the rectum and even more frequently for inflammatory bowel disease, such as colitis. In an ileostomy, the colon (and, in most cases, the rectum) are removed, and the end of the small intestine is rerouted. A permanent opening (a stoma) is created surgically in the abdominal wall; waste from the small intestine empties through the stoma and is collected in a soft pouch worn on the abdomen and emptied when convenient.

16. See *Little Women, Rose in Bloom*, or any other novel by Louisa May Alcott. Also, note the frequent expressions of shame in Tolstoy, Dostoyevsky, Turgenev, and Chekhov.

17. Helen Merrell Lynd, *On Shame and the Search for Identity* (New York: Harcourt, Brace, 1958), pp. 19, 27–35.

18. Similarly, for a single person, *I can no longer expect to be loved*; to a mate who has been mutilated, *You are no longer what I loved*; to oneself, *I am no longer what I loved*.

19. Andrew C. von Eschenbach, M.D. and Dorothy B. Rodriguez, R.N. M.S., E.T., eds., *Sexual Rehabilitation of the Urologic Cancer Patient* (Boston: G. K. Hall Medical Publishers, 1981).

20. Based on a manuscript by Dorothy B. Rodriguez, who is program director of the Enterostomal Therapy Education Program at University of Texas M.D. Anderson Hospital and chief of the Enterostomal Therapy team there. Much of this material appeared as two columns "Loving cannot be taken for granted" (6 January 1980) and "Love, intimacy and cancer" (13 January 1980). Reprinted with the permission of Dorothy Rodriguez and Universal Press Syndicate.

Chapter 11

1. Arnel Van Gelder, Elizabeth Arden, Chicago.

2. Not to be confused with insisting that a dying person not die. See page 125.

3. This is not the same as immunotherapy, which is not even a standard therapy for any cancer at this time, though methods to evaluate it are underway. Immunotherapy attempts to augment, with tumor vaccines and newer preparations such as Interferon, the body's own response.

    That immune systems can be altered is a concept of O. Carl Simonton, M.D., who feels that augmentation of the immune system can be triggered through imaging—a technique of visual imagery borrowed from biofeedback techniques. Dr. Simonton may be correct, but I object to the basic notion that you're really in control if only you're strong enough and follow his imaging techniques faithfully. The implication is that, if Dr. Simonton's rather simplistic imaging techniques do not work, the patient has failed to do them properly. This is as questionable as Dr. Simonton's premise, stated as a fact, that there are cancer-prone personalities, that all of us who have cancer have it because we were so discouraged, defeated, and depressed by our life situations that cancer somehow was the only solution. If this were true, psychiatrists and psychoanalysts could cure cancer, but so far neither the American Psychoanalytic Society nor any of its members have made any such claim.

4. Norman Cousins, *Anatomy of an Illness as Perceived by the Patient* (New York: W. W. Norton, 1979), p. 37.
5. Ibid., p. 44.
6. Ibid., p. 45.

Chapter 12

1. Norman Hugo, M.D., was the first physician to suspect my cancer was metastasizing. Had he not immediately gotten me into the hands of oncologists, I would not be here now.
2. From "On Her Child's Death," a Japanese haiku by Kaga No Chiyo, tr. Curtis Hidden Page, in *The Case for Poetry: A Critical Anthology*, 2nd ed., ed. Frederick Gwynn, Ralph Condee, and Arthur Lewis (Englewood Cliffs, N.J.: Prentice-Hall, 1965), p. 144. Mr. Page's translation actually reads as follows: "I wonder in what fields today / He chases dragonflies at play / My little boy who ran away."
3. There are no guarantees. The right to die is an extremely complex ethical and legal issue, still unresolved in our highest courts. Concern for Dying, an educational council, can provide information on "living wills": Concern for Dying, 250 West 57th Street, New York, New York 10019. (See chapter 8, note 26, for a list of states that have passed legislation establishing the conditions under which such documents are legally valid.)
4. Philippe Ariès, *Western Attitudes Toward Death: From the Middle Ages to the Present*, tr. Patricia M. Ranum (Baltimore: Johns Hopkins University Press, 1974), p. 11.
5. After the Reformation, last rites assumed a lesser importance, except for Roman Catholics.
6. *Western Attitudes Toward Death*, p. 63.
7. A usually erroneous presumption that has been well documented by virtually every thanatologist or other investigator of death and dying. See Hans O. Mauksch, Ph.D., "The Organizational Context of Dying," in *Death: The Final Stage of Growth*, ed. Elisabeth Kübler-Ross (Englewood Cliffs, N.J.: Prentice-Hall, 1975), or David

Dempsey, *The Way We Die* (New York: McGraw-Hill, 1977), pp. 67–68.

8. Jessica Mitford, *The American Way of Death* (New York: Simon & Schuster, 1963), p. 204.

9. "Even if you cannot choose the manner of your dying, you can choose to think about the way in which you will die and perhaps change it a little bit so that it is more acceptable to you and to your loved ones." Edwin Shneidman, *Voices of Death* (New York: Harper & Row, 1980), p. 184.

10. I Corinthians 15:8–10.

Index

Abandonment
  of dying patient in pain, 82
  feelings of, 18–19
  at time of diagnosis, 4, 5, 8,
    96
  See also Discrimination;
    Insensitivity
Advanced Cancer. *See* Cancer,
  advanced
Advocacy organizations, 24–25,
  85–86, 136, 144, 145 n.4
Aides. *See* Hospital personnel,
  aides
Alcohol, 81
Alternative to Mastectomy, An
  (Graham), 150 n.12
American Cancer Society, 24,
  47, 54, 86, 144, 152 n.8
American Psychiatric Society, 86
American Psychoanalytic Society,
  156 n.3

American Way of Death, The
  (Mitford), 126
Analgesics. *See* Drugs; Narcotic
  analgesics
Anatomy of an Illness (Cousins),
  117–18
Anesthesia, early, 80–81
Anesthesiologists, 80, 83
Anger, 3, 6, 9, 11, 15–26, 35,
  51, 57–58, 64, 92–93,
  97–98, 117, 138, 151 n.3
  justified, 24, 35, 151 n.3
  lessening of, 9
  as normal reaction to cancer,
    15
  release of, 19, 25–26, 98
  suppression of, 25, 97–98
  targets for, 25–26, 64
  used to effect change, 16–17
  See also Fury; Outrage; Rage;
    "Why me?"

quadrantectomy, 150 n.14
radical, 44, 150 n.14
segmental, 143
supraradical, 55, 148 n.5
and uninformed consent, 52
See also Breast cancer; Surgery,
radical
Maurer, Dr. Helen, 31
M. D. Anderson Hospital and
Tumor Institute, 109
Medical education
contemporary treatment of
neoplasms, 50
Continuing Medical Education
(CME) seminars on pain, 84
courses needed in human
sexuality, 102; in
humaneness, 40; in pain
relief, 86
"how to tell" and "when to
tell," 39
in medical ethics, 39
Medical equipment, 16–17, 46,
48, 145 n.2
Medical ethics
courses in, 39
and doctrine of informed
consent, 55–56
and suffering, 71
and withholding diagnosis, 30,
33, 37
See also Informed consent
Medical knowledge, gaps in,
140, 149 n.6
See also Medical education
Medical oncologist. See
Oncologist, medical
Medical schools, 39–40, 83, 86,
102
See also Medical education
Medical students, 16–18, 32, 37,
39, 152 n.6

Medication. See Drugs
Medicine, art of, 70
Memorial Hospital, 74–75,
105–6
Memorial Sloan-Kettering
Cancer Center Pain Service,
76
Merrill, Dr. John M., 61, 64–66,
69, 86–87, 137–40
Metastases. See Cancer, metastatic
Methadone, 72
See also Narcotic analgesics
Methodism. See Religion,
Christianity
Michelet, Jules, 78
Middle Ages, 81
See also Dark Ages
Million, Dr. Rodney R., 143
"Mind-cure optimism," 79–80
Mitford, Jessica, 126
Montague, Dr. Eleanor D., 142
Morphine, 72, 86
See also Narcotic analgesics
Morticians, 126
Mourning, 13, 119, 149 n.7
See also Grief; Loss
Mutilative surgery. See Surgery,
radical

Narcotic analgesics
fear of creating drug addiction
with, 72, 74, 80, 81
inadequate use of, 72–73
misconceptions about, 71–76
and non-narcotic drugs, 84–85
proper use of, 73–74, 80
in street use, 74
timed schedule, 87
See also Drugs
National Cancer Institute, 33,
45, 84, 94, 144, 145 n.1,
147 n.1, 152 n.8